My Life in Football

By Sir Bobby Charlton and available from Headline

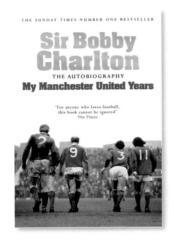

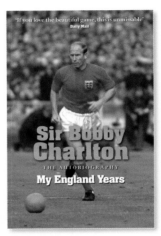

My Manchester United Years

My England Years

My Life in Football

Sir Bobby Charlton

with Ivan Ponting

headline

First published in 2009
by HEADLINE PUBLISHING GROUP

2

Cataloguing in Publication Data is available from the British Library

ISBN 978 0 7553 6181 6

Typeset in Baskerville and Perpetua by Perfect Bound Ltd

Printed and bound in Great Britain by
Butler Tanner and Dennis Ltd

Headline's policy is to use papers that are natural, renewable and recyclable products and
made from wood grown in sustainable forests. The logging and manufacturing processes are
expected to conform to the environmental regulations of the country of origin.

HEADLINE PUBLISHING GROUP
An Hachette UK Company
338 Euston Road
London NW1 3BH

www.headline.co.uk
www.hachette.co.uk

Contents

To the great game of football;
and to the memory of Bobby Robson,
a cherished friend

Foreword

by Ryan Giggs

If anyone had the slightest doubt about the enduring monumental stature of Bobby Charlton in world football – and given his unparalleled achievements in the game, really it's hard to conceive why that might be the case – they should watch him any time the Manchester United party arrive at a ground, or check into an airport or hotel. Instantly he is besieged by a milling crush of autograph hunters, all desperate to capture his signature, and it's not uncommon for the queue confronting Bobby to be far longer than those attending current high-profile members of the team.

Everywhere we go he is held in a respect bordering on awe, and it seems to me that his time is never his own. Yet invariably, and despite being one of the most modest men I have ever met, he copes brilliantly with the ceaseless attention, even at the end of a long, tiring journey. As a young player growing up at Old Trafford, perhaps travelling to tournaments in Europe, you are taught how to behave in public, how to handle yourself in close proximity to fans who can sometimes be quite lively, and Bobby personifies the right way, the Manchester United way. He is the ultimate ambassador for our club and for all of sport, and I view it as a huge honour that I've been asked to contribute a few scene-setting words for his book.

Being a United supporter as I grew up, I had always revered the name of Bobby Charlton, but I'd never come into contact with him until I had a trial with the club when I was 13. I was playing in a game on one of the many pitches at Littleton Road, near The Cliff training ground, when suddenly I noticed that Alex Ferguson was watching, then the next minute my eyes boggled as I spotted Bobby Charlton walking over. It was kind of surreal to see a United legend and the club boss watching me and the other lads playing football. I thought: 'What are they doing here?' Of course, this was just before the manager knocked on my door and invited me to sign for United, which I didn't waste a moment in doing.

As the years went by, with Bobby being around the club as a director, I gradually got to know him and to realise what a gentleman he is. As for his United appearance record, I never dreamed that I would ever get anywhere near it; such a far-off pinnacle just didn't occur to me. You set yourself different targets as you progress. First you want to get into the team, then you want to stay in the team, and you don't look into the distance at all. The record wasn't mentioned to me until a couple of years ago, but even when it was drawn to my attention it was never anything I was particularly striving for, not something that was foremost in my mind. I suppose I was always too taken up with the next game to dwell on it, though as the milestone finally hove into view I realised what a colossal honour it would be.

The way I got there was fairy-tale stuff, equalling Bobby's mark on the last day of 2007/08, when I managed to score the clinching goal as we beat Wigan Athletic to retain the title. As if that wasn't dramatic enough, I set the new record by coming off the bench in Moscow on the night we won the Champions League. If that's not fantasy made real, then really I don't know what is.

The next few hours were unforgettable as the celebration back at our hotel roared on towards the dawn. But then as I was sitting at a table having a couple of drinks with my wife and my mum, suddenly the music stopped and the club's chief executive, David Gill, came to the mike. He asked all the players to step on to the dance floor – with the exception of Ryan! What was going on? It all became clear as David made a little speech about me, then Bobby stepped up to add a few flattering and typically generous words before presenting me with a beautiful watch engraved with the number 759, my total of games for United. Of course, that was the cue for all the lads to start singing and chanting my name, and taking the mick mercilessly. Now there's a surprise!

I have been fortunate enough to have experienced plenty of fabulous moments during my long career, but honestly this was one of the very best. To be honoured by such a magnificent footballer and truly gracious person as Bobby Charlton, one of the all-time masters of the world game and a man with Manchester United in his heart, exceeded even the most far-fetched fancies of the little lad he had watched scampering around at Littleton Road more than two decades earlier.

I think it's a tremendous idea to tell his story in pictures and Bobby's reflections offer a fascinating extra dimension. I'm sure you'll enjoy it as much as I did.

Ryan Giggs,
October 2009

Introduction

This book is essentially a scrapbook of my life. Assembling the pictures for it, and summoning up the words to complement these images, has been both a joy and a privilege.

The process has lifted my heart because it has rekindled so many cherished memories, of friends and comrades and loved ones, of days and nights shot through with glory, of occasions ingrained indelibly on the consciousness of the countless millions to whom football means so much.

Then there are the less tangible but, to me, equally vivid aspects of my years in the game. At the most down-to-earth level, there are the sights and sounds and, yes, the smells of the dressing room. Rather more rarefied, there was running out to the thunder of the crowd at Old Trafford, my Theatre of Dreams, or at dear old Wembley, which might have been a flawed and ageing beauty but which once boasted the finest playing surface in the world and an atmosphere that was all its own. There was facing the challenge of going to work in the howling cauldron of Hampden Park, or at the Bernabeu, or Anfield or Highbury; the incessant striving for that perfect pitch of fitness required to serve my club and my country; the constant travel, much of it mundane but some of it exciting and stimulating; and always the camaraderie, the banter, the bonds that no passing of years can break.

Of course, there has been pain, too. The Munich air disaster claimed the lives of 23 people, including eight Manchester United footballers, among them some of the best and closest pals I have ever known. Even at the distance of more than five decades, during which my life has been crowded with more good things than any individual could reasonably expect, the consequences of that calamity on a slushy Bavarian runway in February 1958 remain with me. They are in my mind every day, and they will never leave me.

It is inevitable, though, that the stark reality of Munich serves enduringly to concentrate my thoughts on the remarkable blessings that I have enjoyed, causing me to ponder for the umpteenth time just how fortunate I have been since falling in love with the game of football as a toddler at home in the narrow streets and cramped backyards of Ashington, the mining town in the North East that was my first home.

In never wanting to be anything else but a professional footballer, I was not alone. It was the dream of virtually every lad I knew. But I was overwhelmingly lucky on two counts. First, I was born into a family immersed in the game – four of my uncles and my mother's cousin, the brilliant Jackie Milburn of Newcastle United, made their living from kicking a ball. Secondly, I was endowed with the natural ability to make my vision a reality, in the process building a career which encompassed all the great occasions while taking me to virtually every corner of the globe, making lifelong friends wherever I went.

But even the quite colossal sum of all that does not reveal the full extent of my fortune. My life in football can be equated to an emotional journey, and one which I could not imagine even contemplating without the unending love and support of my wife, Norma, and the rest of my family.

When I muse on this personal treasure, it becomes ever more important to me with the passing of time that I can give something back, even though I could never come remotely close to repaying all that I have received. I've got a name, a reputation, in different parts of the world and I try to use that to help some of the wonderful causes that I hear about all the time, those which save lives or provide money, or make difficult lives better, particularly for the next generation.

I appreciate that people will listen to me if I seek an audience. Nobody ever puts the phone down, even politicians, and that's too great an opportunity to miss. When I travel with United, usually I find something else to do in the countries we visit, maybe call at an orphanage or attempt to spread awareness about crucial issues, such as the crying need to reduce the impact of landmines in such scarred locations as Cambodia and Bosnia. Then again, I am also involved with organisations on our own doorstep, such as the It's A Goal project, aimed at dealing with depression among youngsters, an admirable crusade started by Macclesfield Town and taken up by other clubs, including United. I suppose I am incredibly busy for someone who has passed three score years and ten, but I don't mind that and I thank goodness that I'm well enough to do it.

Between these covers I have attempted to let the photographs tell their own story . . . my story. To amplify further, I have appended my own reflections, together with some generous contributions from many of those whose paths I have crossed. Not for the first time, and I trust not the last, I am inclined to conclude that my luck has known no bounds.

Bobby Charlton,
October 2009

Above It's a story that might have been conceived and written in football heaven. This is the night Ryan Giggs played his 759th game for Manchester United, thus beating my club record and helping to win the Champions League into the bargain. Pandemonium reigned as the players and coaching staff, with their families and friends, celebrated through the early hours of an uproarious Moscow morning following that nerve-shredding victory over Chelsea, but we found a moment of comparative tranquillity to spring a surprise on Ryan. With Alex Ferguson looking on like some benevolent godfather, I handed our unassuming Welshman an inscribed watch to mark his personal achievement. I certainly wasn't sad about losing my record. I knew it would be overtaken one day and I could not have chosen a better man to do it. I have had the pleasure of watching him develop since his arrival as a little lad two decades ago, and always he has epitomised all that is right about United. He remains as polite and modest a person as you could ever wish to meet, a wonderful advertisement for our club and the game. And what a talent.

Alex Ferguson:

Without question Bobby Charlton is the greatest Manchester United player of all time – and that's saying something! I know Ryan Giggs has beaten his record, and that's phenomenal: it's right to marvel at that. But there are a lot of benefits Ryan gets which Bobby didn't, such as the sports science, the increase in pace and fitness, the nutritional stuff. There weren't substitutes throughout most of Bobby's days, and teams didn't have huge squads. In comparison, Ryan's been nursed, especially in the last few years. Having got into the team at 17, he never played every week, he was monitored very carefully and he was subbed sometimes, which has all helped him to carry on with his great, great career. Certainly I wouldn't dream of taking anything away from the fantastic footballer that Ryan has been and remains. But Bobby played every week on pitches which were nothing like they are today. Then there are his staggering achievements. He's still Manchester United's highest scorer, and England's; he collected what was then a record number of caps; he was European Footballer of the Year, and he was at the heart of United throughout the period of their most emblematic change, from 1958 to 1968. For my money, Bobby Charlton is absolutely without peer in the history of the English game.

CHAPTER 1

Early days — from East to West

Above This is the first team I ever played for, and I've got two reasons for being as pleased as punch as I sit proudly in the middle of the front row. The first is the silverware I'm clutching after the Hirst North A Juniors – known as the 'Doonies' as we inhabited the downstairs section of our red-brick school in Ashington, Northumberland – had just won our local schools competition and I was captain of the side. The second is the beautiful new crimson-and-black strip we were wearing, a far cry from the ragbag of white odds and ends we had been used to. I'll never forget the day our headmaster Mr James Hamilton (that's him on the left) got me to model it. He had me running into the classroom while singing the signature tune to *Sports Report*. I was too happy to be embarrassed as I delivered those immortal strains – Da-da, da-da, da-da, da-da, da-dadda-da-da-da-da – at the top of my voice. It raised a cheer which would have done justice to the Stretford End in full cry. Maybe shouting the loudest was Alan Lavelle, on my left – that's me with the cup in the front row. He was the toughest player in the team, and I was the second toughest because I was his pal! He was a centre half, while I played anywhere and everywhere. In those days you just chased the ball, although our terrific sports master, Mr Norman McGuinness (right), did his best to impose some order.

Opposite This reminds me irresistibly of what it was like to grow up in the decade after the Second World War. It was an immutable rule that if you did something of importance – in this instance being picked for England Schoolboys for the first time – then you had to have your picture taken formally. At that time people didn't walk around with cameras in their pockets – the word digital meant something to do with your fingers! So I was taken along to a photographer's studio, and everything had to be just so. I was delighted that the FA allowed me to keep the shirt, and I still treasure the cap, but I haven't seen the certificate for half a century. I can still recall vividly that first game for England Schoolboys against Wales, particularly walking out at Wembley in front of 93,000 screaming supporters, mostly kids who had made bus trips from all over the country. I could scarcely believe they'd allow us to play on that exquisitely manicured surface which I knew would suit my passing game perfectly. I was in paradise. The game went well for me, as I scored twice in a 3–3 draw. The next day our house was besieged by scouts from league clubs, and my life changed forever.

Left It wasn't only the talent scouts who descended on our terraced miner's cottage at 114 Beatrice Street, Ashington, shortly after my Wembley debut for England Schoolboys. The newspapermen arrived, too, all wanting to rig up daft pictures of my family kicking a football in the backyard. This one shows my brothers – ten-year-old Gordon and Tommy, who was seven – in an unlikely scrimmage for the ball with my mother and myself. Our Jack would have been in the picture, too, but he'd already left to join Leeds United. Not that any of us minded posing for the camera; it was all a bit of a novelty.

Opposite Naturally enough, the press scented a story when they discovered that my mother had four brothers who had played league football, and that she was a cousin of Jackie Milburn, the shining star of Newcastle United. Beyond that, they weren't slow to realise that she wasn't one to shrink from the limelight. Sure enough, when somebody came up with the notion that she had taught me to play football, which made a nice headline even if it bore no relation to reality, she was happy enough to go along with it. It didn't bother me. True, it felt faintly ridiculous to be posing for some of these photographs, but it wasn't doing me any harm. Looking back, this shot of my mother and myself in a heading duel was perhaps the oddest of them all, not least because we both appear to be giving absolutely everything we've got to win the ball. Who came out on top? Well, it looks as though I might just have sneaked it but I don't think it was a classic effort. And just look at the lace on that ball! It stood proud of the surface and if you didn't meet it properly it could cut you badly. To tell the truth, I'm not sure my heading ever improved much down the years. I suppose I did manage the occasional goal (I remember one in particular at Wembley in May 1968 . . .), though none as a kid. As for who taught me to play, in all honesty I think the game just came to me naturally, but if I had anyone to thank it would be my grandfather Tanner Milburn, my uncle Tommy and Mr McGuinness at school. Still, my mother always wanted me to be a professional footballer, the game was in her blood, and I will always be grateful to her for all that encouragement.

Jack Charlton:

We realised that Bobby was going to be a bit special as a player when he was about five years old. He was always kicking a football or a tennis ball against a wall, and when it bounced back it stuck to him like a magnet. Everybody in Ashington knew he was special. They all said he would play for England, and he did.

Above Here's a good quiz poser, and I don't reckon there's too many who will come up with the answer. At which Premier League ground did this England Schoolboys team beat the Republic of Ireland 8–0 in April 1953? The answer is Fratton Park, Portsmouth, now cosily enclosed by stands, but mostly open to the elements more than half a century ago. Happily it was a beautiful spring afternoon when we faced the Irish, though clearly the pitch had endured a long, hard winter. That's me in the white shirt on the extreme right of the front row. The skipper with the ball at his feet is Wilf McGuinness, and on his right is Jimmy Melia, who went on to play for Liverpool and win two full caps, while the goalkeeper in the middle of the back row is Tony Hawksworth, who helped United to lift the FA Youth Cup in three successive seasons but made only one senior appearance.

Opposite Scrubbing my kit after my two goals at Wembley? Well, yes, but only to please another of those insatiable photographers. Just after the war we had a big barrel in the yard and all our washing went in there. Next to it was a hand-worked mangle to squeeze it dry, and my mother looked after the entire operation. But never let the facts get in the way of a good yarn . . .

Opposite Jackie Milburn was my second cousin and my hero, and I loved him dearly. When he scored with this glancing header against Manchester City in the first minute of the 1955 FA Cup final, it shocked the Geordie nation because he didn't score many in the air. But this was a really classy effort from a perfectly judged connection after running off his marker at the near post. I saw it on television at our house with Eddie Colman and Wilf McGuinness, who were in Ashington for the weekend. In those less rabidly partisan days, because they were from Manchester they both wanted City to win, while my family was supporting Newcastle. The whole street went mad when Jackie scored. A Powderhall sprinter, he was renowned for his speed and when he accelerated he was like a torpedo powering through the water. People bounced off him, too, because he was so strong. Jackie and I were very close, and right up to the time he died in 1988, whenever I went to Newcastle United he'd be waiting to meet me. He loved the fact of me being a footballer, and often he joked with me about my employers, but he wasn't upset that I didn't go to St James' Park. He understood that Manchester United were in my heart and there were no hard feelings at all. He was a marvellous man and I miss him to this day.

Left As a lad I was a Newcastle supporter, but that didn't stop me from being seduced by the skills of the greatest players in the land. The brightest star of the day, the most famous by a distance, was Stanley Matthews (above left), who exuded an aura that was all his own. You always felt you couldn't take your eyes off him in case he did something special. He used to tease full backs mercilessly, as he is doing here with poor Joe Walton of Preston. Often Stan would walk up to them slowly while staring into their eyes rather than looking down at the ball between his little bandy legs. His touch verged on the supernatural and always he knew exactly where that ball was. His agitated opponent would be waiting desperately for him to make his move, but the instant Stan noticed the defender was even slightly on his heels, he would be gone, gliding effortlessly over the ground like a deer in full flight. He could go either right or left, and over those vital first ten or 15 yards he just couldn't be caught. Stan's speed and skill made your hair stand on end. If ever he got clobbered, which was rare, the foul always looked so obvious.

Then there was Tom Finney, the 'Preston Plumber' (below left), another winger of sublime talent but a sturdier and a more complete all-rounder because he was also blindingly impressive at centre forward or in midfield. What they had in common was complete control of the ball and awareness of what was going on around them. Unquestionably they would have been top performers in any era.

Above I never cease to marvel at this shot of United's 1955 FA Youth Cup-winning line-up because it emphasises so graphically the gargantuan stature of Duncan Edwards, the best footballer I ever played alongside. Obviously that's Duncan standing on the extreme left, and the rest of us look like pygmies beside him. We had just clinched the trophy with a 3–0 victory at West Bromwich, in which both he and I scored, thus triumphing 7–1 over the two legs. I keep saying what a fantastic player he was and some people look at me in half-disbelief, maybe thinking I'm laying it on too thick. But, genuinely, he was unique, an absolute colossus in terms of both talent and physique. There were days when he literally dominated games, seemingly in possession of the ball for 30 or 40 per cent of the time. When I was a schoolboy I thought I was really good at football – and then I saw Duncan Edwards. Pictured at The Hawthorns are, left to right back row: Duncan, Terry Beckett, Shay Brennan, Tony Hawksworth, Alan Rhodes, John Queenan. Front: Peter Jones, Denis Fidler, Eddie Colman, Wilf McGuinness, myself.

Above Look at those turn-ups on my jeans! I'm not sure they were exactly the height of fashion, but they were all I could get and I was happy with them. My United team-mates Eddie Colman (left) and Wilf McGuinness were staying with me for a few days at Beatrice Street in Ashington, and we were joined for this snap outside the back door by one of my younger brothers, Gordon. Eddie was from Salford and Wilf was a Mancunian, and both came from fantastically warm and friendly families, who welcomed me into their homes on a regular basis when I moved down from the North East. So when the season was over my parents invited them to visit as a bit of a thank-you.

Right Many a time early in my career there would be a cameraman on the pitch shortly before kick-off to take action pictures. His work would turn up all over the place – particularly in comics like *Tiger*, on bubble-gum cards or in the two main magazines of the day, *Charles Buchan's Football Monthly* and *Soccer Star*. We had to go through the motions, with a full follow-through just for the photograph. One thing's for sure – I could never be so relaxed if I was really shooting at goal in earnest. This picture screams that it was taken in the 1950s. Just look at the boots. They were of terrible quality, awful things, often lumpy and uncomfortable, nothing like the 'slippers' the players wear today. I'd be given a pair of boots in July and was expected to make them last the whole season. The groundstaff boys looked after them for us, but if I went to play for England I would take them with me and had to clean them myself. Have times changed? Just a bit!

Below right Bright-eyed and Brylcreemed, ready for my career to begin taking off in the autumn of 1956.

Opposite Scoring a goal on my Manchester United debut was something I had dreamed about incessantly, yet when it actually happened it was more exhilarating than anything I could have imagined. There was this wonderful rush of euphoria as the ball went in. I never wanted the moment to end, and in a sense it didn't because I can recall it still with gratifying clarity. It was October 1956 and I'd been longing for the 'Old Man', as Matt Busby was known, to call me into his office to tell me I'd been picked. Finally, ahead of the home game with Charlton Athletic, he sent for me, but even then I feared my hopes would be dashed as he was clearly anxious about my right ankle. It was three weeks since I had gone over on it, suffering strained ligaments, and it was still sore, but there was no way I was going to miss this opportunity so I assured him it was fine. At last I was in, and with the adrenaline whizzing around my system I didn't feel a twinge from the moment the game got under way. Johnny Berry gave us an early lead, and then along came my chance. The ball reached me on the left corner of the box at the old Scoreboard End, and I hit it instinctively with my left foot past 'keeper Eddie Marsh. It nestled beautifully (if I say so myself . . .) just inside the far post and I turned away, arms raised in ecstasy, as team-mate Billy Whelan and Charlton defenders Cyril Hammond (left) and Jock Campbell looked on. Later I scored a second from a similar position and we won 4–2. It was a perfect day.

Roger Hunt:

I was in the Old Trafford crowd when Bobby made his debut against Charlton, and I was as impressed as everyone else by the potential he revealed that day. At the time I was supposed to be playing for my local team, Stockton Heath, but our game had been called off so a few of the lads decided to watch United instead. Bobby scored a couple and generally made a fantastic impact, fully justifying all the great things I had heard about his exploits for England Schoolboys. I thought I'd missed the boat after Bury had not offered me professional terms, and I could hardly have dreamed that our paths were destined to cross in the way that they did. I went to the celebration of the 50th anniversary of his debut, and he was amazed when I told him I'd been there for his big day half a century earlier.

Above This was only the second time that my big brother Jack and I had played against each other as professional footballers. It was before the game at Elland Road in March 1957 when United were closing in on the title and Leeds were ensconced safely in the top half of the table. There was absolutely no antipathy between us because we were on opposite sides; we were always totally supportive of each other. More than anything else it was an extremely proud moment for both of us and for our family. After all, you don't get brothers playing in the top division very often. Before kick-off he'd have said something like, 'Are you all right, Kidder?' and we'd have wished each other luck. As it turned out, we won 2–1 with Johnny Berry and myself scoring our goals. Mine was the late winner, a header from a corner, but Jack wasn't marking me directly so they couldn't blame him.

Jack Charlton:

What was it like to play against my brother? My mother used to come and see us more often than not when we were playing each other, and she used to tell me to leave the little 'un alone. He nutmegged me once and he ran away from me. I chased him but I couldn't catch him. Don't know what I'd have done if I had!

Above Significantly Jack's the one with the rod and line as we perch on the salmon bridge at the River Wansbeck in Ashington. We used to go there in the school holidays, but while my brother was an expert fisherman, I contented myself with a bottle containing a bit of bread, hoping some unwary minnow might take my bait. I just liked being there, looking into that lovely, clear, unpolluted water. I wonder what it's like now. The next chance I get, I'll go and have a look. Northumberland has a spectacularly beautiful coastline yet it's never had the plaudits it deserves and most people haven't explored it. Perhaps the folk there are happy to keep it to themselves!

CHAPTER 2

Titles, trailblazing and tragedy

Above I've heard of the Busby Babes, but this is ridiculous! A local four-year-old joins the United players for training just behind the seafront at Blackpool in preparation for our 1957 FA Cup semi-final encounter with Birmingham City. That's me in the foreground making heavy weather of my squat-thrusts, with Wilf McGuinness behind me, Eddie Colman at the back and Geoff Bent on the left. We always stayed at the Norbreck Hydro Hotel – which I recall had the best shower I'd ever experienced – and we used to joke that Matt Busby and Jimmy Murphy must have had shares in the place. In fact, it was ideal for us, as we used to do a lot of stamina work along the coast. Interestingly the back gardens of the houses are not lined with onlookers as they would be today. We were never irresistible objects of fascination to the public in that era.

Opposite Here's a period piece – my mum and dad listening to an FA Cup draw on the family radiogram. No doubt the shot was staged for a local photographer, who would have asked for the snap of me to be perched on the cabinet.

Right To play football with the original Busby Babes was a glorious experience, but to call them my friends was an even richer privilege. This was a night out at the Midland Hotel in central Manchester after United had beaten Birmingham City in the 1957 FA Cup semi-final at Hillsborough. As usual our big, laughing cavalier of a centre forward, Tommy Taylor, was at the heart of the fun and he just couldn't resist a blow on the saxophone, which had been borrowed from one of the terrific musicians who often made a celebration at that venue a particular delight. Dubliner Billy Whelan (left) is often characterised as being a serious individual, and so he was where his football was concerned, but he knew how to enjoy himself too. Next to him is Wilf McGuinness, one of my oldest pals in football and certainly the loudest, as he spends a great deal of his time talking at the top of his voice. Wilf and I started work together at Old Trafford on the same summer day in 1953. On the right, seemingly bent on drowning Tommy's solo by pouring beer into his sax, is dear David Pegg, like Tom a lovely lad from Yorkshire. As for me, that looks like a distinctly sloppy salute. Obviously I didn't learn a lot during my two years of National Service.

Wilf McGuinness:

The first time I encountered Bobby we were both not long out of short trousers. He was captain of East Northumberland and I was skippering the side from Manchester in the English Schools Trophy. Bobby remarked that soon we'd be seeing each other again at the trials for England, but I was a slightly older hand, having played the year before, and not having seen him in action I was inclined to be sceptical. My first thought was: 'Do you really think we will? And who are you exactly?'

Of course, I found out pretty quickly. Before long we both joined United and despite our obvious differences – he was inclined to be quiet and I, um, wasn't! – we became good pals and remain so to this day. People who might think they know him, but actually don't, have often slated him for being aloof, but that's absolute piffle. He might have been a tad shy in his younger days, but when he's with people he trusts he can be tremendous fun – a terrifically kind person who really loves children. So don't be taken in by that serious expression. Bobby Charlton's a smashing lad – and what a footballer.

Right My dad's still got the Birmingham City match programme in his pocket as we enjoy ourselves after our FA Cup semi-final victory. Dad was never a football man, and he knew he didn't know much about the game, but the way he used to support Jack and myself was marvellous. He had married into a football family, but he didn't pick up too much down the years. He was happy just to watch, then go out to work, and he worked hard. Above all he was glad that we were doing well at something we enjoyed and which didn't involve joining him in the pit.

Below I don't know what Dad and I are chuckling about here, but certainly it isn't the finer points of the game. We were always really close, and he was proud of what Jack and I had done, but sometimes I think he wondered what all the fuss was about.

Opposite Duncan Edwards takes the steering wheel after volunteering for grass-cutting duty at the Bernabeu? Not exactly. This was a photo opportunity engineered for the Spanish press ahead of United's European Cup quarter-final against Real Madrid in April 1957. Duncan's assistant groundsmen are, left to right, Colin Webster, myself, Billy Whelan and Eddie Colman. I was there only as a reserve and watched the match from a seat high on the rim of that vast concrete bowl, a vantage point from which I was utterly captivated by the genius of Alfredo di Stefano, who masterminded Real's 3–1 win like a general on a battlefield. Before that I had never imagined that one player could influence a game in such an all-embracing fashion. He was everywhere, totally in charge from first whistle to last.

Above This is the group of fantastic footballers who lifted the league championship for the second successive season in 1956/57. Many of these lads are household names but one, Johnny Doherty (second from right in the back row), never had much luck. He was a gifted, extremely intelligent inside forward, a visionary passer and very cute with his work on the ball. Sadly his development was halted by a succession of horrendous knee injuries which culminated in premature retirement. Back row, left to right: Colin Webster, Wilf McGuinness, Jackie Blanchflower, Johnny Doherty, Eddie Colman. Middle row: Tom Curry (trainer), Bill Foulkes, myself, Freddie Goodwin, Ray Wood, Billy Whelan, Mark Jones, Duncan Edwards, Bill Inglis (assistant trainer). Front row: Dennis Viollet, Johnny Berry, Matt Busby (manager), Roger Byrne (captain), Jimmy Murphy (assistant manager), Tommy Taylor, David Pegg.

Right I had been playing for East Northumberland Boys against Jarrow and Hebburn Boys on a pitch frozen as solid as concrete. At the final whistle a dapper little man tiptoed his way across the jagged ruts and asked me a big question: 'When you leave school, would you like to join Manchester United?' It was the talent scout Joe Armstrong, who was a born charmer. Later there were about 18 clubs inquiring after me, and we listened to all of them, but Uncle Joe – everybody called him that – was the first and he had sown some very persuasive seeds. It was important to us that he hadn't come *after* I had scored twice at Wembley for England Schoolboys, that he'd made it his business to find out about me before the storm of publicity blew up. He taught me so much, and not only about football – for instance the rudiments of speaking in public. Even now I'm not cocky and confident as a speaker, but at least I'm not afraid of it and I've got Joe to thank for starting me off. Here we're celebrating after a United win in 1957.

Above I can't deny that it was one of the pleasures of my life to find myself part of the ritual championship celebration shot in the communal bath at Old Trafford in April 1957, but I never felt I was an integral part of that particular title triumph. I was only a young lad at the time, used mainly as a reserve, and I counted my lucky stars that I had accumulated enough appearances to qualify for a medal. Matt Busby looks delighted, and obviously he was, but he was never one to jump up and down at moments of success. He was always in perfect control of himself. Those in the water are, left to right, Johnny Berry, Bill Foulkes, Billy Whelan, Eddie Colman (drinking from his mug), David Pegg, Tommy Taylor (standing at back) and myself. Skipper Roger Byrne is yet to take the plunge.

Opposite This is how I'll always remember Duncan Edwards – genial, relaxed, but with a characteristic quiet certainty about him which proclaimed that he knew he was a great player. Yet for all that charisma, and his habitual majesty on the park, Duncan was a delightfully modest and friendly lad. But what about that training gear? It was tatty and basic, with not the slightest concession to fashion. What today's footballers would make of it I shudder to think.

Above Tommy Taylor is falling over backwards as his header loops into the Aston Villa net to bring us fleeting hope in the 1957 FA Cup final. I'm waiting for any rebound, but I wasn't needed. Our centre forward's goal was a defiant gesture with only seven minutes left, but we couldn't force an equaliser and lost 2–1. We were already crowned as league champions and were hot favourites to become the first club in the 20th century to lift the league and FA Cup double, so defeat was a crushing blow. It came in bitterly controversial circumstances, as Villa's Peter McParland had collided with our 'keeper Ray Wood, resulting in a serious injury to Ray which meant, in that unenlightened era before substitutes were permitted, we had to soldier on with ten men. These days, McParland would have been sent off following such an incident, but he was able to add insult to injury by scoring both Villa's goals. It didn't alter our belief, though, that we were the best team in the country.

Above Three carefree lads who wouldn't have wanted to be anywhere else in the world than in Longford Park, Stretford, on a sunny Sunday morning, chatting happily after taking in a local game. I tended to be the listener because David Pegg (centre) and Tommy Taylor were older than me, with far more first-team experience. The three of us seemed to hit it off from the start, probably because we all came from mining communities and our dads were all working underground. We never stayed away from football for long. If we weren't playing it or watching it then we were talking about it. We didn't play on Sundays in those days but loads of games were going on in the park and all our digs were near. The delightful thing was that people didn't fall over backwards to notice us. It was the same on Saturday nights when we used to meet, often in The Bridge pub at Sale, now long gone. It was all very relaxing, and looking back it seems such a gloriously innocent time. Tommy and David were both lovely outgoing people with strong Yorkshire accents and we became very close. I was devastated when they lost their lives at Munich and I still keep in touch with their families.

Above Imagine . . . eight young footballers living under the same roof. Do you reckon we had some fun? Just a bit! These digs were at Ravenscroft Road, about 100 yards along from Old Trafford cricket ground, and Mrs Watson, the lady on the left with the big smile, looked after us rather well. From the smart way we are dressed here, I would guess that we are having a quick meal before heading out for the evening to celebrate; maybe it is somebody's birthday. Going clockwise from the left foreground, the players are Tommy Taylor, myself, Billy Whelan, Jackie Blanchflower, Mark Jones, Gordon Clayton (part hidden), Alan Rhodes (with only his back in view) and Duncan Edwards. We left this house some time before the Munich tragedy, when Mrs Watson and her husband stopped running the business. It was a shame because we all had to split into ones and twos, though I was happy enough with Billy at a place on Great Stone Road.

My brother Jack is the genial host as Manchester United arrive at Elland Road for a First Division encounter during those golden freewheeling days before Munich. Joining the Charltons, no doubt for a spot of friendly banter, are Wilf McGuinness (left), Ray Wood (second right) and Duncan Edwards (right). After the game, most likely, I would have linked up with Jack for a bite to eat and a pint. Early in our careers we often went to watch each other play, but then life got more hectic because of European competition and those meetings just drifted away.

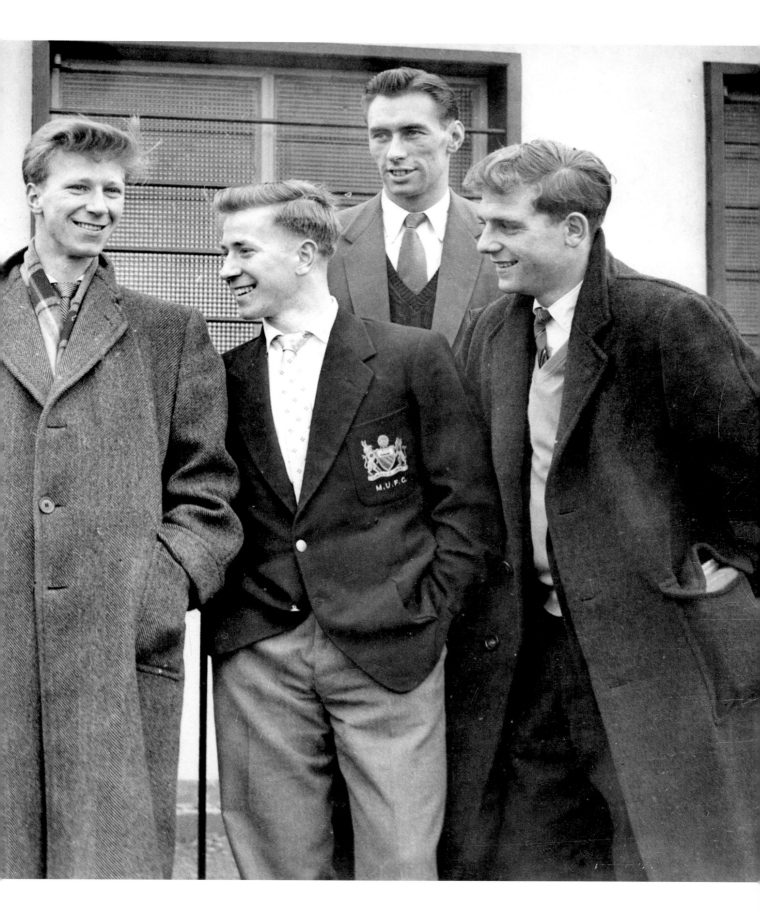

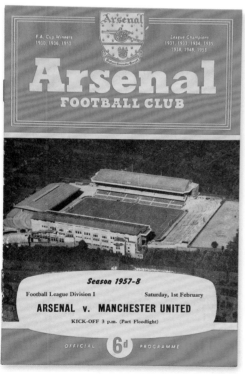

Opposite The famous Highbury clock shows five to three as Duncan Edwards writes his name for a young admirer. It's unbearably poignant to reflect that it must have been one of the last autographs he would ever sign as this encounter with Arsenal on a Highbury mudbath proved to be the Busby Babes' farewell game on English soil. Duncan was always very patient with kids, though it was unusual to encounter them on the pitch so shortly before kick-off. There would have been no pitch invasion back in the 1950s, so I suppose the lads in the picture were being given a treat.

Above The Arsenal match took place only five days before the Munich air disaster and ever after has been referred to with reverence as a fittingly enthralling epitaph for our fantastic young team. We won 5–4 but not before the scoreline had see-sawed crazily. United led 3–0 at the interval, Arsenal fought back to 3–3, then we stretched out to 5–3 before they made it a cliff-hanger by scoring with a quarter of an hour still to play. Our star that day was left winger Albert Scanlon, who positively skated over the quagmire, setting up one goal for me and tormenting Arsenal right back Stan Charlton (no relation) to distraction. This was a chance which squirmed away from me, but the relief on the faces of Arsenal 'keeper Jack Kelsey, the prone Stan, and defenders Jim Fotheringham and Gerry Ward (on one knee) suggest that it was a close shave.

Above Running out in Belgrade on the afternoon of 5 February 1958, a little more than 90 minutes away from reaching the European Cup semi-finals, but just a day away from unthinkable disaster. Leading the way is Dennis Viollet, followed by myself, Kenny Morgans, Mark Jones and Albert Scanlon.

Opposite top This is a study in total concentration, absolute focus. We're lining up to face Red Star Belgrade in Yugoslavia with a place in the last four of the European Cup at stake, and the mind of every player is given over completely to the job at hand. Just look at that bank of fans behind us. They were screaming very noisily, but none of them were rooting for United. We took no supporters with us, we were utterly on our own. But then look at Duncan, our man-mountain, on the left of the line. He is radiating confidence, his body language declaring there was no way we were going to lose, and that must have been immensely intimidating for the opposition. The rest of the players, from left to right, are Eddie Colman, Mark Jones, Kenny Morgans, myself, Dennis Viollet, Tommy Taylor, Bill Foulkes, Harry Gregg, Albert Scanlon and Roger Byrne. Are we ready or not? Come on!

Right Red Star's pitch was a treacherous mixture of slush and mud, but as a forward that suited me because it made life nightmarish for defenders. Already 2–1 up from the Old Trafford leg, we scored three more before the break, Dennis Viollet grabbing the first, then I skidded one in from distance before putting away this chance from close range. They rattled us with three in the second half, but we hung on for a deserved win. After that we were looking forward to going home . . .

Right The numbingly desolate scene which sums up the catastrophe which overtook Manchester United on the afternoon of 6 February 1958. As night falls and snow continues to descend from the heavens, our plane lies broken in the Munich slush. We had been on the verge of conquering Europe, but mere sporting considerations ceased to matter as the cruel reality of lost lives began to sink in.

Below There was nothing much wrong with me physically when I woke up in the hospital at Munich after the crash. The bandages on my head offer a different impression, but I had suffered nothing worse than concussion and some minor cuts. Precisely what was going on in my mind, though, was another matter. When this was taken, probably on the day after the accident, I had found out exactly who had died from a young German in the next bed. But hearing what had happened, and actually grasping the enormity of it, proved to be two different things. In fact, my mind was reeling as I struggled to find some sort of reality, and that rather vacant half-smile for the cameraman masked a desperate feeling of confusion.

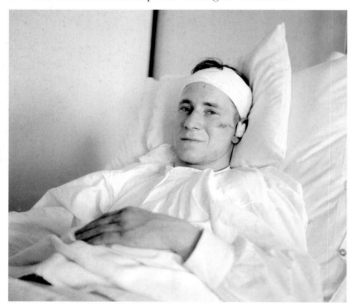

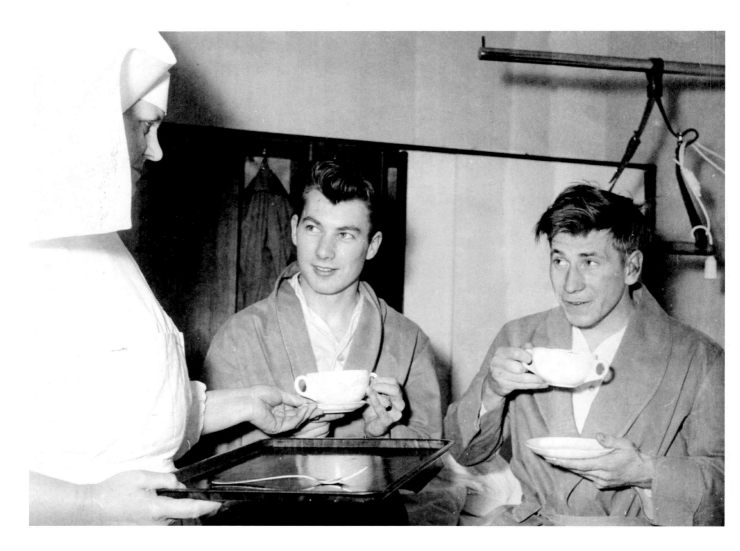

Above Like me, Kenny Morgans appeared to have escaped lightly in terms of outward injuries, but although we always tried to produce a smile for the nuns who looked after us so attentively in the hospital, in truth we were wandering around like lost souls in some impenetrably dark fog. Kenny was a lovely young lad and a gifted right winger who had recently got into the side at the expense of that tough, talented and vastly experienced performer, Johnny Berry. It's fair to say that the young Welshman's promise had appeared to be boundless but, distressingly, after the accident he was never the same player. The tragedy had taken something away from Kenny and he never regained that exciting early impetus, instead drifting away to the lower divisions. He still comes to every Munich-era reunion, though, and everyone is always delighted to see him.

Above and left At first glance this might be the happiest of scenes, Bobby Charlton back home in Ashington enjoying a kickabout with his young neighbours and seemingly having fun acting out the Pied Piper of Ashington. But behind my cheery expression is a world of grief and pain. I had just returned to Beatrice Street for a brief period of recuperation after losing so many of my friends at Munich, and was persuaded to pose for these pictures by pressmen seeking the latest angle on the story of Manchester United's struggle to battle on in the face of unprecedented adversity. I understood that they had their jobs to do so I was ready to oblige them, even if I didn't feel like it. In retrospect, though, I'm impressed by some of the kits on display. It wasn't so easy to find replica shirts back in 1958.

Above I'm one of the gaunt-faced spectators, along with assistant manager Jimmy Murphy (above right) and physiotherapist Ted Dalton, at the most emotional match ever played at Old Trafford. Nearly two weeks had crawled by and United were in action for the first time since Munich, facing Sheffield Wednesday in the FA Cup. The ground was packed to the rafters and the atmosphere verged on the hysterical as we ran out 3–0 winners. I felt sorry for the Wednesday lads; they were on a hiding to nothing, with what seemed like the entire world willing United on to victory. Dad and my Uncle Tommy had driven me down for the match, and that night it dawned on me that it was time to go back to work. I was fit enough and I felt it would be ridiculous to return to the North East when I should be out there battling alongside my pals. My mind was made up, as I think you can gauge by my expression.

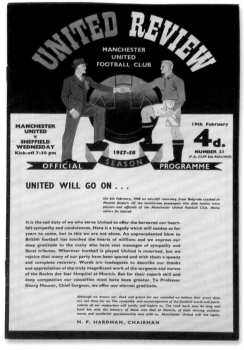

Above I'm thwarted by West Bromwich 'keeper Jim Sanders as I strive to break the deadlock in our FA Cup quarter-final replay at Old Trafford in March 1958. But after making my post-Munich comeback in a 2–2 draw at West Bromwich in the first match, eventually it fell to me to set up the only goal of that unbearably tense rematch. It was very late in the game when I picked up the ball on the right, knocked it past their full back and hit a hard, low cross which Sanders didn't claim, enabling Colin Webster to side-foot into the net. I was almost overcome with relief because I didn't think we'd have prevailed in a third meeting. That night it felt like all the raw emotion in which Manchester had been awash since the accident was concentrated on the pitch, and when the final whistle went I felt as limp as a rag.

Left Relaxing with Colin in the wake of victory. The Welsh international was a sparky front-man, a little toughie always ready to put his foot in. He contributed some important goals to the United cause, but none more crucial than his winner against Albion.

Above At first glance, there is something incongruous about this picture. Why is a Manchester United footballer in full kit indulging in a kickabout on what looks like a public park at the bottom of somebody's garden? The answer brings back an avalanche of memories for me, some tragic, others life-affirming. It was the spring of 1958, some three months after the calamity at Munich had claimed so many lives and made some of us wonder how in heaven our club could carry on. Yet somehow, and gazing back down the years it still seems like a miracle, we had reached the FA Cup final, in which we were to meet Bolton Wanderers. Such was the level of grief and commotion still raging in Manchester that Jimmy Murphy – who was still doing such an inspirational job in charge of the team while Matt Busby continued on his tortuous road to recovery from the injuries he had suffered in the crash – decreed that we had to get away from it all, and he took us to Blackpool. We were based at the Norbreck Hydro Hotel, a comfortable retreat where we found at least a modicum of peace, and we trained on this strip of grass just along the road. Usually we would have been in tracksuits and jumpers, but on this sunny morning we had dressed up for a photo call. Even at a distance of more than half a century, it still seems a trifle surreal.

Left Matt Busby was still in excruciating pain from his injuries suffered at Munich, but nothing was going to keep him away from his team as we undertook our training at Blackpool ahead of the FA Cup final against Bolton in May 1958. He appeared very frail as he leant on his stick, holding himself gingerly with his poor back clearly hurting horribly, and I could hardly believe how tough he was to put himself through such an ordeal. I felt so much compassion for him, too, because of the responsibility he so plainly shouldered for the boys who had died. That reaction was a natural one, perhaps, but he had no need to feel guilty because he had made the right decision for the club when he had spurned the warnings of the domestic authorities to begin blazing the British trail across Europe. He was still on his stick at Wembley and, as usual, he was smiling, though I'm absolutely sure he was smiling through the pain. Matt Busby remains one of the most remarkable men I have known.

Left Without the fire and the passion and the inspiration of Jimmy Murphy, United would never have made it to Wembley in 1958. Matt's number-two worked a veritable miracle in leading such a patchwork side to the FA Cup final after the depredations of Munich and Matt Busby's fight back to health. The club owed Jimmy a massive debt for keeping United's flag flying during that dark period of our history. Here is Jimmy (centre) in typical mode, jabbing a finger and clenching a fist to ram home a point. Invariably he was right, and no one had a more meaningful influence on my career. Also listening intently is little Ernie Taylor, the veteran schemer who arrived as an emergency signing after the crash and helped our young players enormously.

Right As one of the United players who seemed to attract publicity, especially after Munich, I was invited on to the hugely popular TV programme *Sportsview* ahead of our Wembley date with Bolton. Interviewing me in the studio was Kenneth Wolstenholme, already pretty much the voice of football even though it was eight years before he uttered his immortal lines at the World Cup final, and there was a live link on a screen with Bolton skipper and my England team-mate Nat Lofthouse. Contrary to some folks' expectations, I was neither nervous nor camera-shy. It was no ordeal to talk about the FA Cup final, football was my business and I always got on well with Nat, who was a terrific centre forward. That said, there was no doubt that his charge on our 'keeper Harry Gregg which produced their second goal was a foul, but that's another story!

Below United captain Bill Foulkes escorts the Duke of Edinburgh down the line before the big game. Players in the picture, left to right, are Ian Greaves, Bill, Alex Dawson, myself, Dennis Viollet grasping the royal hand, Ernie Taylor and Freddie Goodwin. Jimmy Murphy is on the end, rightly taking his place alongside the team.

Above Bolton full back Tommy Banks knew how to tackle, and it looks like he managed to nick the ball away from me in this challenge at Wembley. The Trotters' defence had a reputation for being tough and there was no doubt that their other full back Roy Hartle *was* hard. As for Tommy, a smashing character and a good pal of mine, he *talked* hard!

Above The incident which might have altered the destiny of the FA Cup in 1958: I bent a shot with my right foot which whacked the far upright, then rebounded into the arms of rooted 'keeper Eddie Hopkinson, with Roy Hartle helpless to intervene. That was a let-off for them, but what made it worse was that they went straight down the other end and scored. Instead of equalising, we were 2–0 down and never threatened them again. Of course, we were disappointed, but what was winning or losing a football match compared to what had recently happened to us? The important thing was that the club had survived and we had proved we could still function at the top level.

Right The face of youth, the face of optimism, the face of a lad looking forward to an evening out in the late 1950s.

Opposite Why are the Charlton brothers grinning like Cheshire cats? Well, it is April 1958 and I have just heard that I have been called up for my first full cap, to face Scotland at Hampden Park. We were walking down Market Street in Manchester when one of us bought an *Evening Chronicle*, which revealed the happy news. That's how it happened back then; the FA did send an official letter but it always arrived late so the newspapers would get in first. Jack was overjoyed for me, as I was for him when he received the summons some seven years later. As for the overcoats, they were warm, smart and only coincidentally similar.

CHAPTER 3

My country's colours

Above Shaking hands with England skipper Billy Wright during a break in training at Somerset Park, Ayr United's ground, ahead of my first England game. In the middle is another debutant, Jim Langley, the Fulham left back, who was always chirpy and terrific fun in the dressing room. I shared a room with Billy, who was supremely helpful and understanding to me at a time when I was still somewhat bemused by what had happened at Munich. He readied me for Hampden, too, explaining that there would be 130,000 screaming fans and none of them ours. Billy was a wonderful man and I owed him plenty.

Right By any measure, it was a dream scenario. I was making my full England debut against Scotland at Hampden Park in April 1958; we were two goals up and Tom Finney had just dashed to the left byline and clipped over the most inviting of crosses. I was eight yards out from the back post as the ball dropped temptingly into my stride, and for a split second I considered a knock-back to Derek Kevan or Johnny Haynes. But then I thought: 'The game's safe, what the hell!' So I volleyed it first time and it flew in. Then, as I ran back for kick-off, I was chased by Scotland 'keeper Tommy Younger, who congratulated me on my strike and said there would be many more to follow. What a fantastic act of sportsmanship! But the

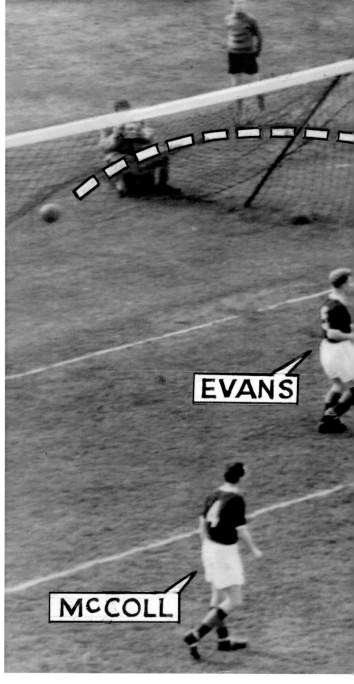

best part of the memory for me is that it was the great Tom Finney, one of my boyhood heroes, who set me up. I love the way newspapers used to mark the ball's trajectory and label the players. I treasure this picture. The only pity is that Tom was out of shot.

YOUNGER

KEVAN

HADDOCK

CHARLTON

HAYNES

DOCHERTY

Opposite England captain Billy Wright was popular with the players and not averse to a spot of horseplay, but there was nothing spontaneous about this particular romp during training at Roehampton. A press photographer was looking for something offbeat, so Tom Finney and I grabbed Billy's arms, while Maurice Setters and another lad, obscured by me, took hold of his legs. And no, we didn't drop the skipper.

Above This is more serious stuff. The two figures flying through the air at Roehampton are myself and Bobby Robson during a high-summer England training session ahead of the 1958 World Cup finals in Sweden. The ground is in south-west London, but had a delightful, almost rural, feel to it. I always liked Bobby, who was a goal-scoring inside forward who became a highly influential wing half. He loved talking about the game, was clearly very intelligent and was an absolute natural to become a manager.

Above I appear to be in sombre mood after arriving back in London after the 1958 World Cup finals in Sweden, having not played in the tournament. Hand on heart, though, I wasn't upset that I hadn't been picked. People told me there was a hoo-ha in the English newspapers about my omission, and obviously I would have preferred to play, but I had no divine right to a place. I was only 20, I had played against Yugoslavia in a warm-up game and not done well, so now I was out. Perfectly understandable. I suppose I was still suffering stress in the wake of Munich, and maybe the strain is showing in my face. But at least I remembered to buy somebody a present!

Opposite top You might think I could hardly believe my luck at finding myself in such exalted company – and you'd be right. We were training at White Hart Lane ahead of our Wembley meeting with Russia in October 1958. Like Bryan Douglas (on my right), I was still very much a new boy in the England set-up,

so it was wonderful to be made to feel a part of things by such stars of the world game as, from my left, Billy Wright, Johnny Haynes, Tom Finney and Nat Lofthouse. Billy's enlightened captaincy was one major reason for the relaxed atmosphere. He wasn't an iron martinet, quite the opposite, but he was a born leader, a man others were ready to follow. Billy, Tom and Nat were all at, or approaching, the veteran stage, but Johnny was much closer to me in age and we got on well together. He was a magnificent inside forward with a tremendous football brain, and receiving a pass from him was pure pleasure. He would play the ball perfectly into your stride with exactly the required weight, and he always played it on the floor. I doubt if he ever hit a hopeful chip in his life. Johnny could get upset if he surrendered possession unnecessarily but, trust me, that didn't happen very often. We had a terrific day against the USSR, beating them 5–0 at Wembley with a hat-trick from Johnny, a goal from Nat and a converted penalty from me.

Right Sometimes the England party met at Bolton to train before heading north to face Scotland, and I wouldn't be surprised if local lad Tommy Banks (left) was advising the rest of us, my United clubmate Wilf McGuinness, skipper Billy Wright and me, to follow the excellent advice on the Burnden Park stand. Dining at the Pack Horse in Bolton could not be recommended too highly and I have made many a happy visit there down the years. Tommy, like Wilf, was always up for a laugh and maybe they were taking the mick out of me. Billy might be gauging my reaction, but I seem to be enjoying the joke.

Above Scoring against Scotland, the 'Auld Enemy', was always a thrill, and this effort at Wembley in April 1959 was particularly sweet because it was the only goal of the game. Earlier I'd made several support runs from deep with nothing to show for it, but this time our right winger Bryan Douglas got to the byline and knocked a beautiful cross into my path. Having lost my marker, I climbed as high as I could, concentrated on heading the ball downwards and saw it sail past 'keeper Bill Brown into the net. I'd been in full flight at the moment of impact and had to launch myself into a roll on landing, which must have looked quite spectacular. You can just spot Bryan on the extreme left of the picture, while the Scottish defenders are Bobby Evans (left) and Eric Caldow. Our coach, Walter Winterbottom, was especially delighted as he was always impressing on us the importance of supporting the man on the ball.

Opposite top left It might have been murder to train in the sapping humidity of Rio de Janeiro during England's summer 1959 tour of South America, but it was worth the effort. I mean, just look at that six-pack! I treated the trip as a fabulous adventure, an exciting step into the unknown, and I wasn't disappointed. It was an incredible experience to run out in front of some 200,000 fanatical supporters at the Maracana. The stadium felt like an entirely alien environment with its moat to keep fans off the pitch – we never had crowd trouble at home back then – and the spongy grass which made the ball pop up unpredictably. If nothing else, it explained why Brazilian footballers had needed to acquire such magnetic control.

Above Shooting practice at Highbury, while training for an England under-23 encounter north of the border in 1960. Balance and timing are all-important aspects of getting the ball on target. Pure power alone is not enough.

Left When the serious business of an England training session was over, usually the players would have a kickabout just for the fun of it, and that was when I might find myself between the posts. People have always said that goalkeepers must be crazy, and I reckon there might be something in that. After all, they've got their own union, they don't talk the same language as the rest of us, and they do a job which I have never envied them in the least. However, I have to say I'm impressed with my concentration level here, with eyes fixed firmly on the ball. Clearly the shot is on the way – I wonder if it ended up in the top corner.

Opposite The scene is Ashington railway station, sometime in the early 1960s. My mother and her cousin Jackie Milburn (centre) have just met the journalist Clement Freud, later to earn considerably more fame as a politician, broadcaster and chef, off a train from London. He had ventured to the North East to write his second article about me, the first having been nearly a decade earlier when I was playing for England Schoolboys. Now the news story was that I had been dropped from the full England team and he wanted to know how I was handling it. Mum and Jackie don't seem too downhearted and neither was I. I reckoned I had the ability to reclaim my place and in due course that's how it turned out.

Above There is no doubt that the central figure in this tableau at an England training session in October 1959 is a certain Brian Clough. Unquestionably he was high on confidence, never short of a word, and if there was a debate going on then he'd be at the heart of it. I played alongside him in both his internationals, against Wales (a draw) and Sweden (a defeat) that autumn. He was at centre forward with Jimmy Greaves and I completing the inside trio, which evidently didn't impress Brian. He declared the pair of us were difficult to play with because we wanted the ball all the time! Taking part in this discussion are, left to right, coach Walter Winterbottom, Ronnie Clayton, trainer Harold Shepherdson, Brian, Tony Allen, Don Howe, Trevor Smith, Maurice Setters, myself, Jimmy and Edwin Holliday.

Above Between October 1960 and May 1961, this England team enjoyed a run of six straight victories under Walter Winterbottom, scoring 40 goals in the process while conceding only eight. Much of the credit, rightly so, went to our skipper, Johnny Haynes, and to Jimmy Greaves, that most clinical of finishers, but I always felt that the great unsung hero in that side was the Tottenham centre forward Bobby Smith. He was a fearless, bustling, old-fashioned leader of the line, never the type to be showered with bouquets by the press, but he didn't half make life easy for his midfielders. Bobby was always showing for the ball and was strong enough to hold it while others ran into position; he was superb in the air and he was vastly underrated when it came to skill. Somehow I always felt safe when he was there. I could never understand why he lost his place, but he was a bit of a rough diamond and maybe he said a word out of place at the wrong time. It was a crying shame.

The line-up was, left to right back row: Jimmy Armfield, Bobby Robson, Ron Flowers, Ron Springett, Peter Swan, Mick McNeil, Brian Miller (usually in reserve). Front row: Bryan Douglas, Jimmy Greaves, Bobby Smith, Johnny Haynes, myself.

Opposite When we beat Scotland 9–3 at Wembley in April 1961, it amounted to the most sensational result in the history of meetings between the two ancient rivals, but I have to admit that scoreline was a bit of a freak. England played well, but there wasn't *that* big a gulf between the two sides. The most eye-catching player on the pitch was our skipper Johnny Haynes, here clutching the Home International trophy as he is carried aloft by, from the left, Peter Swan, Jimmy Armfield and Mick McNeil. At the time he was the most influential footballer in the country and this game was made for him. When the Scots went behind, their shape broke down and they began charging everywhere, enabling Johnny to pick out the gaps with his pinpoint passing. At one point early in the second half, the score was 3–2 and the game was in the balance, but then he took over and they collapsed. I was the only English forward not to score, but I managed to set up one or two. For Scotland, who fielded great players such as Denis Law and Dave Mackay, it was truly the stuff of nightmares, while for us it offered a memory to cherish into old age.

Opposite You can't relax in front of 100,000 people at Wembley. That was vividly evident when England faced the Rest of the World to celebrate the FA's centenary in October 1963. Usually such gala contests, with nothing concrete at stake, don't amount to much. But when you are faced by the likes of Alfredo di Stefano, Eusebio and Ferenc Puskas, not to mention such fiercely proud Scots as Denis Law and Jim Baxter, there can be no half measures. OK, the players weren't kicking each other up in the air, but the game was decently competitive with plenty of entertaining football for the purists. We won 2–1, and here I'm attempting to swerve past a defender who is just out of shot.

Above This was the worst game I ever played in – and I'm not blaming the dog. England needed to draw with Bulgaria to reach the World Cup quarter-finals in Chile in 1962 and we played safe, progressing after a goalless bore. That really incensed me, provoking the only argument I ever had with our captain, my friend Johnny Haynes. I contended that if we wanted to proclaim to the world that we were potential winners – and I believe we were as good as anyone in the tournament, maybe barring Brazil – this was no way to go about it. Bulgaria were no great shakes, but they did go close once, and it could have been a disaster. Johnny accused me of moaning unnecessarily after we had made the last eight, but I felt strongly about it. As for the dog, he had his tail between his legs – obviously he wasn't too impressed, either.

Above Garrincha was a magician, and he knocked us out of the 1962 World Cup virtually on his own. The Brazilian winger with the oddly bent legs used the same trick every time. He dropped his left shoulder and his marker had to react, but then Garrincha darted suddenly to the right and he was gone. As you can see, I was no better at stopping him than anyone else. We lost our quarter-final 3–1 in Viña del Mar and he was absolutely electric. He was tiny but he outjumped big Maurice Norman to head the first, Vava nodded the second from a rebound from his free-kick, then Garrincha swerved in the third from 25 yards. I thought we matched Brazil in most respects, but he was the difference. When they made Garrincha they broke the mould.

Opposite It's a peculiar thing. When I was a footballer, records meant nothing to me, but long after I retired I began to take a slightly different perspective. This was my 31st goal for England, which took me past the benchmark laid down by those two all-time greats Tom Finney and Nat Lofthouse. It was October 1963 and we were at Ninian Park, Cardiff – it couldn't be anywhere else with that huge ad for Captain Morgan rum on the roof of the stand. The ball came into the box, I ran on to it and got in a shot which was saved by Dave Hollins, but the ball bounced back to me and I managed to convert. Leading up to the game I'd not thought of the record until prompted by journalists, and even then I wasn't bothered. After all, scoring goals was what I was picked for. I was just doing my job. Even three decades later, when Gary Lineker got very close to my tally of more goals scored than any other Englishman, I wasn't concerned in the slightest. But then, when he fell one goal short, I surprised myself by feeling really pleased. Even so, I thought back to a chat I'd once had with Ferenc Puskas. I'd mentioned to him Pelé's recent astonishing feat of registering his 1,000th goal. The Magnificent Magyar's reply? 'I scored my thousandth about eight years ago!' So, on reflection, perhaps I shouldn't get too excited about my 49 for England . . .

Right The Charlton brothers of England . . . it had a lovely ring to it, and I couldn't have been happier for Jack when he was called up for his first cap to face Scotland at Wembley in the spring of 1965. Yet I must admit that the moment he gave me the news fell a trifle flat. He found out he had been picked as he came off the pitch at the City Ground, Nottingham, after Leeds had beaten Manchester United with a late goal in an FA Cup semi-final replay. Naturally he was a happy man when he stuck his head round our dressing-room door to tell me, but we were still hurting from the defeat and one of our lads piped up with: 'Sorry if we don't jump up and applaud!' Of course, I put my disappointment to one side and congratulated him. I'd been expecting his selection because he thoroughly deserved it. He was never a stylish player, some people called him clumsy, but my goodness he was effective, and he was as game as a pebble.

Jack Charlton:

When I got into the England team, Our Kid was already settled into the job and he and Bobby Moore looked after me marvellously. I used to sit with them on the bus and they used to tell me where we were going.

Opposite 'OK Kidder, this is how we'll beat Scotland.' Brother Jack was overjoyed at his England call-up, but he was never overawed at the prospect of playing on the international stage. He always had a sharp tactical brain, as later he demonstrated during his successful time in management, and here I'd guess he was coming up with some devilishly cunning plan during a training session ahead of our meeting with the Scots. Characteristically, some might say, he is in relaxed mode with his socks round his ankles at the end of a morning's work, while mine are neatly tied. I was always more comfortable like that.

Right Alf Ramsey is scratching his head as he strolls across Wembley's lush green carpet with Jack and myself, but I assure you it wasn't because he was at a loss about how to approach the forthcoming meeting with the Scots. The England boss was a supremely organised coach who paid attention to every detail, and also he was an extremely practical man. That's why he called up Jack and Nobby Stiles to make their debuts in this match. They weren't glamorous players, but they were winners, and all Alf was interested in was the result.

Above When Denis Law hit the target, as he did against England at Wembley in 1965, he was a study in undiluted glee and the fans gloried in his celebrations. He was one of the greatest Scottish footballers of all time – some would say *the* greatest – and I couldn't have been happier when he joined Manchester United. He was an inspirational and ferociously committed performer – you'd certainly rather play with him than against him, and that's an understatement! Here he's about to be hugged by another of my club mates, Paddy Crerand (left), and Rangers winger Willie Henderson.

Opposite Denis looks amiable enough as he and I exchange shirts at the end of the game, but he wasn't always quite as friendly. The first time we met on an international field, he clattered me. As I got up I mentioned to him that he'd gone in a bit strong, and he rasped in reply: 'This is not Manchester United – this is for Scotland!' Of course, he was a Scottish hero and that's how he was expected to be. I had no problems with

that, and there were no hard feelings after any game between our two countries. Neither of us were too unhappy after this one, because we'd both scored in a 2–2 draw, though maybe England could claim a moral victory because we'd finished with only nine fit men. Our 'keeper Gordon Banks might be looking for his Scottish counterpart, Bill Brown, for a similar swap.

Denis Law:

The first thing I did when Scotland played England was to forget Bobby and Nobby were my United team-mates. I had to get that out of my mind because for that day my job was to beat them. I never liked playing against them, but I had to get on with it. For that 90 minutes we were rivals; when it was over we were the best of pals again. Did we injure each other? You'd have to ask Bobby that! I don't think he ever kicked anyone. That was never his way. Now with Nobby, it would be a different ball game altogether!

CHAPTER 4

Rising from the ashes

Right There was something about Matt Busby that put people at their ease. It helped that he had an amazing memory for faces, even of people that he had met only fleetingly, and his avuncular Scottish brogue was somehow reassuring. I don't remember this occasion just after Christmas 1958 in the dressing room at Villa Park, but it was typical of the Boss that he was making his young visitor feel welcome. Maybe the lad had won a competition, or had been ill, or perhaps he was related to someone at Villa. Whatever, I'm sure he treasured the autograph Matt was about to sign for him, and his memory of a special moment.

Right When I first met Stanley Matthews – I think it was at a Footballer of the Year dinner, or possibly a PFA meeting – I was in so much awe of him that I could barely speak. When I was a schoolboy, he was very much 'The Man', the ultimate celebrity as far as I was concerned. Once, before a match at Newcastle in which he was to play for Blackpool, he strolled across the pitch and stopped to talk to someone near where I was standing, just over the touchline. I could barely believe that I had seen Stanley Matthews in his everyday clothes, looking no different from anyone else! When I got to know him a little, he turned out to be a real gentleman, and an active member of the players' union. He was still the big star, and his support was crucial in the battle to lift the maximum wage.

Opposite Birthdays are for enjoyment, but also a time for taking stock. As I lit the candles on my 21st, back home in Ashington with the help of my mother in October 1958, I could reflect on a career with Manchester United and England that was well under way, but one over which the shadow of unspeakable tragedy had fallen. This picture appeared in *Charles Buchan's Soccer Gift Book*, and later turned up regularly in the scrapbooks of autograph hunters.

Above This was the first pre-season photo call after Munich, and it was impossible not to look along the benches and think of the lads who would have been there beside us but for the crash, some of the best friends I would ever have. But life didn't stop, Manchester United had to go on, and the three survivors of the accident pictured here, myself, Bill Foulkes (centre) and Dennis Viollet, all had to play their part in rebuilding the club. Bill was an old-fashioned, hard-as-nails defender who might have been carved out of granite. If he tackled you in training then, believe me, you would feel the bruises for days. As a working miner – he was only a part-time footballer when I first knew him, sometimes turning up for training still black-faced from his shift – he had to be tough, and that rubbed off on his game. Dennis was a complete contrast, a thoroughbred performer and an instinctive goal poacher, as sharp as a stiletto in the box, but because he didn't carry a spare ounce of stock he was more vulnerable to injury than some. Both were key members of the team before the accident, and were even more important afterwards.

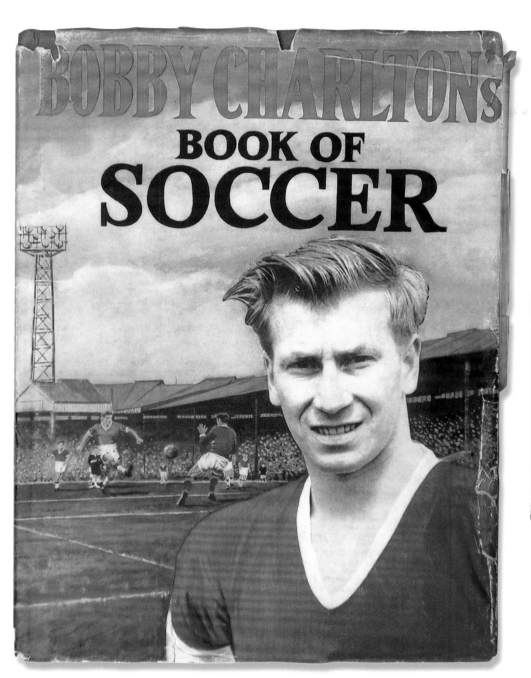

Above left Oh, this takes me back. It was my first literary venture, in 1960, and it was part of a series with racing driver Stirling Moss, cricketer Peter May, Pat Smythe, the show jumper, and flier Neville Duke. It told my life story to that point, and it was intended mainly for youngsters, with plenty of pictures. I guess the cover might ring a bell with a few who were in short trousers around that time.

Above right In the wake of the Munich air disaster, I began to see my face on magazine covers, but although I was never an extrovert exactly, it didn't throw me. Even then I was well aware of Manchester United's position in the world. Because I had survived the crash in which so many household names had lost their lives, people were interested in me and I could understand why.

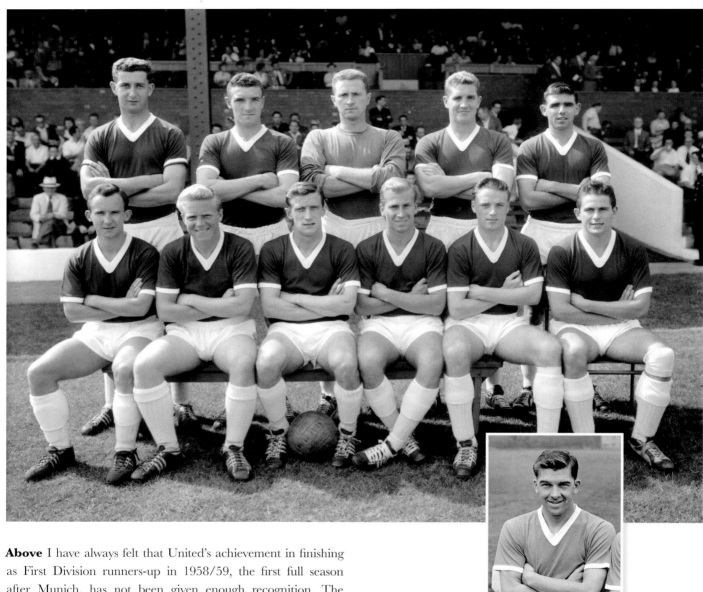

Above I have always felt that United's achievement in finishing as First Division runners-up in 1958/59, the first full season after Munich, has not been given enough recognition. The club had been devastated by the disaster and yet we ended up within six points of the champions, Wolves, although I admit there was never a real likelihood that we were going to win the title. Somehow Matt and Jimmy had put together a pleasingly balanced team: Harry Gregg had been voted the best goalkeeper in the previous summer's World Cup; the defence was strong and intelligently organised; and we scored more than a century of goals. In fact, that was my own most prolific campaign, with 29 strikes. We would not have been able to maintain that impetus without the major reconstruction which followed, but it was some effort in the circumstances. Back row, left to right: Freddie Goodwin, Bill Foulkes, Harry Gregg, Ian Greaves, Joe Carolan. Front row: Warren Bradley, Albert Quixall, Dennis Viollet, myself, Albert Scanlon, Wilf McGuinness. Inset: Ronnie Cope.

Left This shot is a curiosity. Probably it's one of the most commonly used pictures of me in the late 1950s, appearing mainly in books and magazines, and I even noticed it on a postcard in the main reception foyer at Old Trafford, being employed as advertising material for MUTV. Yet there's something amiss – can you spot the mistake? Here's a clue. In those fondly remembered but sadly far-off days when I needed a parting in my hair, invariably it was on my left. Here it is on my right. It hasn't bothered me in the slightest, but someone has entered it into the agency's archives with the image reversed, which gives a marginally off-kilter slant to my features. These days, of course, it wouldn't happen because the sponsorship logo on my chest would give the game away – and unfortunately there'd be no parting to offer the necessary hint. For anyone still in doubt, the correct version appears below.

Above This is a picture, taken during a derby clash with Manchester City in February 1959, which moves me deeply. With the brooding sky and the factory chimney, there is a certain starkness about the scene, but it screams to me of how Old Trafford used to be. Just look how they squeezed the people in! That brickwork tower, and two others visible from the pitch but now long dismantled, offered a vivid reminder that just along the road was Trafford Park, the largest industrial estate in Europe. So many of our fans worked there and that was a huge motivation to Matt Busby. He used to tell us that they slaved away all week, they were subjected to enough boredom behind the factory gates, and that what they craved on Saturdays was excitement. He dinned into us that it was our job to entertain them, to give them a lift, and we took that on board. The atmosphere, with the closeness of the crowd and the glowering backdrop, was astonishing. The darkness above the heads of

City full back Bill Leivers and myself was partly due to the weather, but also owed plenty to the smog. Smells pervaded the ground and we always knew what had been on for lunch in Trafford Park. Spotted dick seemed to be a favourite! The chimneys were an important part of our home advantage, too, because they provided landmarks to the players, who might glimpse them briefly in the heat of the action and know exactly where they were on the pitch. It's amazing to reflect that United's state-of-the-art, three-tier North Stand now occupies this space. It is a truly magnificent structure, but occasionally my mind drifts back, and I know that the image of Old Trafford's past will never leave me.

Above right Flying through the air on either side of me, strictly for the camera rather than in a genuine training exercise, are Dennis Viollet (left) and Johnny Giles. We're at a sports field in Stretford, only five minutes from Old Trafford, which we used often during the early 1960s, especially for pre-season work. Dennis must go down as one of the great names in United history, and I believe Johnny could have, too. He was deeply intelligent, always a thinker, and he was a sublimely gifted passer who saw openings before most others. There was a formidable strength about him, both physical and mental, and I thought it was a shame when he left in 1963. I never really fathomed out why. Perhaps he'd had enough of playing on the wing, and certainly he blossomed luxuriantly as a midfield play-maker at Leeds, but I don't see why he couldn't have been integrated into our side. There's always room for a player of Johnny's exceptional talent.

Johnny Giles:

Bobby Charlton was the best player I ever played with or against, and the most beautiful to watch. Yet despite all the praise and accolades he has received down the years, sometimes I think he is actually underrated among United fans. A recent survey had Eric Cantona down as the greatest United player of all time, but I guess that's a generation thing. For me, Bobby stands alone, both in terms of his natural ability and of the way he conducted himself on and off the field. As an ambassador for the club and the wider game, he has never put a foot wrong.

I'd like to mention the late Dennis Viollet, too. He was another wonderful footballer. Unfortunately for him he was at his peak when the England team was picked by a selection committee and he received only two caps. But he was brilliant, either as an inside forward supporting Tommy Taylor before Munich, or as an out-and-out centre forward after the crash.

Above Whoever said it was better to travel hopefully than to arrive was not a footballer. That aspect of the game has never been anything like as glamorous as most people imagine, with long periods being spent hanging around in airports and railway stations. I visited many countries during my playing days, but saw only a handful of the sights. In fact, I'd been in football for 20 years before I even bought a camera. Killing the time with me here in a station café in 1960 are, left to right, Harry Gregg, Shay Brennan, Wilf McGuinness and Maurice Setters.

Right Have you seen my socks, Dennis? Not the least of the changes that have swept through top-level football in modern times have been to the dressing rooms. Now players can find just about every facility their hearts could desire – state-of-the-art medical and fitness equipment, warm-up rooms, sockets for their hairdryers – and in most cases there is plenty of space. All that's in stark contrast to the days when I was making my way in the game. We used to be squashed into tiny areas, often with only one hook each for all our clothes. Jockstraps, underpants, towels, just about anything would go missing, eventually turning up in a muddy tangle under someone else's seat. At Old Trafford we were lucky in that we had hot-water

pipes, but it was cold enough to freeze your extremities at some of the grounds, though Dennis Viollet and I don't appear to be shivering in this shot. But despite everything, I suppose you could say that the primitive facilities fostered camaraderie. We were all in it together and we would have a laugh about it.

Above As the 1960s began, it was wonderful to see Matt Busby back in a tracksuit. Though he still suffered a great deal of pain, he had recovered substantially from his Munich injuries and was throwing himself into building a new team. For a time he was happy with this inside trio of Albert Quixall (left), Dennis Viollet and myself. Albert, a British record £45,000 signing from Sheffield Wednesday, was a clever play-maker who passed the ball beautifully, while Dennis was a phenomenally sharp striker. He would feint to shoot, his marker would lunge, Dennis would wriggle into half a yard of space, the defender would be off balance and *then* our wiry centre forward would hit it. He was an artist, and that's why he still holds United's league scoring record for a single season, with 32 goals in 1959/60.

One sunny autumn afternoon in 1960 when everyone else had gone home after training, I had my eyes opened to a revolution that was going on in the development of football boots. I had signed what I think might have been my first sponsorship deal, something which was far less common in those days, with the Bozeat Boot Company, which hailed from a little village near Northampton. They introduced me to moulded soles, which were based on the same principle as farmers' wellies, but scientific advances made them much lighter. They turned out to be excellent for playing on hard ground, and I loved wearing them. What a treat – shiny new boots, complete with their distinctive four white stripes running down the sides. I made a few hundred quid into the bargain, and that was a lot of money at the time.

Above On the run but surrounded by Tottenham defenders at White Hart Lane in August 1961. The reason for the unfamiliar colours is that I'm playing for an FA XI, actually the current England team by another name, which was facing Spurs in the Charity Shield after Bill Nicholson's lovely, free-flowing side had become the first in the 20th century to win the league and FA Cup double. Right back Peter Baker is about to make a tackle, while centre half Maurice Norman closes in from the left. That afternoon Tottenham bolstered their aura of omnipotence by winning 3–2 – helped by Bill Brown saving my penalty – and just to complete my day my car broke down on the way home.

Right My miserable expression reveals that United have just been beaten by Spurs in an FA Cup semi-final at Hillsborough on a grim, grey afternoon on the last day of March 1962. Mind, for a bunch of lads who have just reached Wembley, they don't exactly appear full of the joys of spring either. There is no sign of crowing or of flamboyant celebration; that wasn't the way in those days. On this occasion, the best team had won; they had a lovely blend and they deserved their 3–1 victory. The Tottenham players are, left to right, Jimmy Greaves, John White (destined to lose his life to a lightning bolt in 1964), Cliff Jones, Terry Medwin and Bobby Smith.

Above On the bench next to Denis Law at our Stretford training ground on one of his first days at work as a Manchester United player in August 1962. When we signed him for a record fee of £115,000, I was overjoyed, because even at that relatively early stage of his career he was already one of the best footballers I'd ever seen. Yet if anything, my sky-high expectations sold him short. Denis transformed our team. Suddenly we had this quicksilver, fearless, absolutely inspirational figure at the spearhead of our attack, scoring goals for fun, battling for every ball against hulking defenders who dwarfed him, and making himself an idol of the Old Trafford crowd. As Denis strutted on to the United stage, the team's confidence began to burgeon and before long the feeling grew that Matt Busby's post-Munich reconstruction had gained unstoppable momentum.

Denis Law:

When I first met Bobby properly after joining Manchester United in 1962, there was a seriousness to him. As one of the senior players in terms of experience, he felt a huge responsibility after Munich. But still he has always had a great sense of humour, which a lot of people don't realise. Sometimes it surfaces in areas you don't expect, and when we meet up we still have a great laugh together.

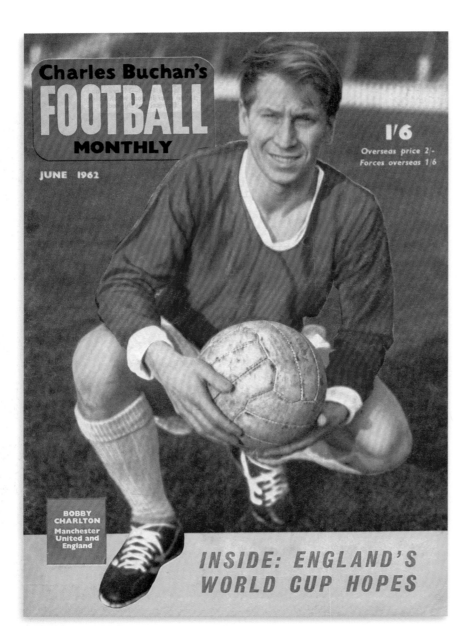

Charles Buchan's

FOOTBALL
MONTHLY

JUNE 1962

1'6
Overseas price 2/-
Forces overseas 1/6

BOBBY
CHARLTON
Manchester
United and
England

INSIDE: ENGLAND'S
WORLD CUP HOPES

Above The best part of half a century after it was published, I still receive copies of this June 1962 edition of *Charles Buchan's Football Monthly* to sign. It was a magazine read by most of the players and it carried credibility because Buchan himself had been a top performer for Sunderland and Arsenal. I know a lot of people would never miss an issue for the world. You knew you'd made it when you made the front cover of *Charles Buchan*.

Opposite If ever a man earned a swig of champagne it was Bert Trautmann of Manchester City, who was the best goalkeeper in the world for much of his career. It was a joy to be asked to play in his testimonial at Maine Road in 1964, and

then to be treated to a spot of bubbly – albeit in tea mugs – in the dressing room afterwards. When we played City, I never tried to place my shots because I didn't want to give myself away, feeling that if I took deliberate aim Bert would know where the ball was going. But in one game, at least, my policy didn't work. I hit a drive as sweet as a nut and, with Bert unsighted by a wall of defenders, it was arrowing for the top corner. But as I was about to celebrate, this hand appeared as if from nowhere to tip the ball over the bar, leaving me slack-jawed in disbelief. He was fabulous at starting attacks, too, with his massive throws – what a performer. Joining him for a drink are, left to right, Bill Foulkes, Denis Law, City's Derek Kevan, myself and Maurice Setters.

93

When we beat Leicester City 3–1 and took the FA Cup back to Manchester in 1963, it marked a telling watershed for United. It was our first trophy since the Munich disaster five years earlier, offering firm evidence that Matt Busby was on the right track. After a long, hard, frozen winter, at the end of which we had only narrowly escaped relegation, we were greeted by a sun-bathed Wembley and I like to think we served up sunshine football to match.

Above I always seemed to be wearing a solemn expression in shots of team celebrations, most likely because I was physically and sometimes emotionally drained at the end of the match. There's no shortage of hilarity from my team-mates, though. Left to right are Tony Dunne, myself, skipper Noel Cantwell, who gave FA officials a fright by hurling the cup skywards, though he did make the catch, Paddy Crerand, who played so brilliantly and emerged that day as a star, Albert Quixall, David Herd and Johnny Giles.

Right I had a hand in our second goal, cutting in from the left wing to get in a pretty powerful shot which my England

pal Gordon Banks could only parry, allowing David Herd to fire in the rebound. The kneeling Gordon's despair is in stark contrast to the glee of the converging United quartet. The scorer is jumping for joy and about to be embraced by Denis Law (number 10), Johnny Giles and myself (number 11).

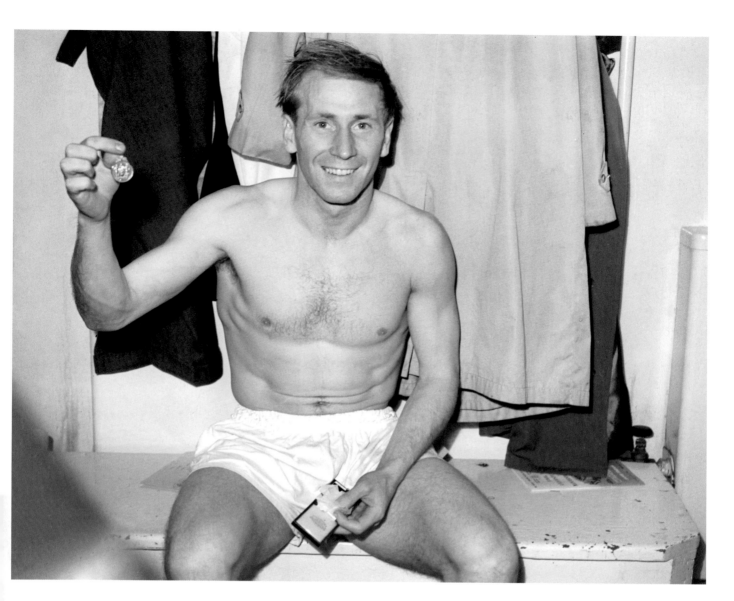

Above The winners' dressing room at Wembley is a deliriously happy place, though by no means as luxurious as the fans might have imagined, witness the chipped paint on the bench. I'm not bothered about the fixtures and fittings, though, as I brandish my precious medal for a photographer. It meant so much to me, having finished on the losing side in my two previous FA Cup finals, on either side of Munich.

Left This time I have no idea I'm in the camera's eye as I enjoy a relaxing drag on a Rothmans, slumping back on my seat and probably re-running the action in my mind. Back in 1963 we had no idea that smoking was such a devastating health hazard, and I'd never touch a cigarette now. Meanwhile David Herd (left), the irrepressible Denis Law (complete with lid) and Maurice Setters just can't let go of that much-coveted silver pot.

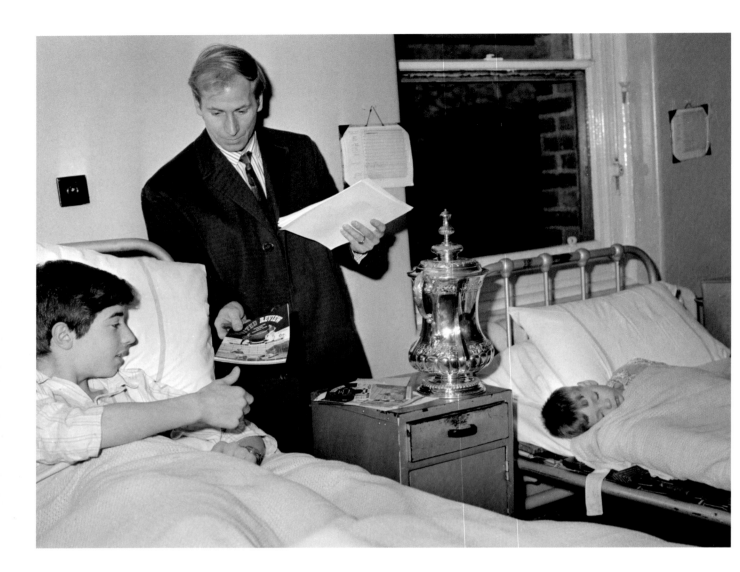

Above This little lad had drifted off to sleep in his hospital bed and missed the United players dropping in with the FA Cup and a few souvenirs in 1963. It's always been a tradition at the club to take trophies out into the local community and this time we visited Booth Hall, now replaced by the absolutely fantastic Manchester Children's Hospital. I was there during the spring of 2009, helping with some fund-raising publicity. It was the occasion of Bob the Builder's tenth birthday and he was keen for us to be filmed together. When I got home my six-year-old grand-daughter, Emma, was on the phone to say she had spotted us. Apparently seeing Grandad with such a star was one of the best things that had ever happened. On the box with Bob the Builder – I was famous at last!

Above United were 3–1 down with only four minutes left of this FA Cup quarter-final against Sunderland at Old Trafford in February 1964. An embarrassing defeat by Second Division opposition was beckoning when a corner came in and I managed to nod it into the net. Their number 5, that excellent centre half Charlie Hurley, who had earlier scored an own-goal, looks disgusted, but worse was to come for our visitors when George Best equalised only two minutes later. The Roker Park replay ended 2–2, with me levelling the scores with another header at the death, before eventually we went through 5–1 in the third encounter at Huddersfield. It had been an epic saga, a breathtaking advertisement for FA Cup football, and we were left to heave a collective sigh of relief at its denouement.

Bryan Robson:

I can always remember the first time I saw Bobby. Even though I was a Newcastle fan, the first game I ever went to, when I was seven years old, was an FA Cup replay between Sunderland and Manchester United at Roker Park, and he headed a last-minute equaliser. He was a tremendous footballer, the type to fire every schoolboy's imagination, and the next time I watched him was on the television, scoring his fabulous goals against Mexico and Portugal in the World Cup.

It's been a great honour for United to offer me an ambassadorial role, now that Bobby is scaling down some of his commitments around the world. With United so popular everywhere, there are just too many places for him to go, too much for him to do. I am aware that I am treading in exceptionally illustrious footsteps and I regard it as an absolute privilege. Not that he's shuffling off the scene. When he speaks he is still so passionate about football in general and United in particular, and it's wonderful the way he stays in touch with the grass roots of the game.

CHAPTER 5

Champions again

It has always struck me that the lot of football photographers, particularly half a century ago, could be a pretty difficult one. I'm ready to stand corrected, but it occurs to me that modern equipment, complete with sophisticated motor-drives and aids to focusing, must make it easier not to miss that optimum split-second of action. I recall cameramen lying on their stomachs, often in puddles or even in snow, waiting and hoping for the right moment to press the button. To get the best shots, they must have had to read the game as well as any player. I'd say the photographers who supplied the two shots on these pages have succeeded admirably, capturing West Ham's Jim Standen diving at my feet in 1963, and Stoke's Mike Bernard contesting a header with me in 1967 on the day we were presented with that season's league title. As for Andy Cowie of Colorsport (right), whose story appears, I can only offer my belated apologies and voice my relief that I didn't scupper his career.

Andy Cowie:

I was a green 18-year-old dispatched to Molineux to cover Wolves taking on Manchester United in the third round of the FA Cup in January 1973 when my rookie career as a sports photographer was almost ended pretty much as soon as it had begun. I had been lectured at length by old hands at my agency, Colorsport, to keep my eye, and my lens, on the ball and as Bobby Charlton was surging towards goal, with me lying uncomfortably on my stomach to one side of the posts, that's exactly what I did.

I was still trying to get used to the pace of the game, which seemed an awful lot faster from my ungainly position, when I found Bobby filling my view with alarming speed. I was clicking away as he loomed very close – and then he let loose with one of his trademark rockets. I clicked again and then – wallop! – the ball rammed the camera, complete with its heavy 400mm lens, right into my eye socket. I was slammed backwards, much

to the delight of the fans behind me, who revelled in what looked like a slapstick sequence, but the harsh reality was that when I was helped to my feet I had lost the sight of my eye.

I was really frightened but didn't go to the doctor until the Monday, when I was told to give it time and I would see again. So I did, although it was a week before my sight returned. I had learned a painful lesson that self-preservation comes before even the most terrific of pictures.

I'm happy to say that was more than 36 years ago and that my career has lasted longer than my film of the game, which somehow disappeared in the confusion surrounding my predicament. Of course, Bobby was in blissful ignorance of my plight, and if I was inexperienced enough to put myself in the path of one of his thunderbolts, that was hardly his fault. I must say, though, that the next time I had the United sharpshooter in my sights, I was extremely careful . . .

Opposite If I'm looking a trifle apprehensive here shortly before kick-off against Arsenal at Highbury, it is misleading. Perhaps I was feeling the cold, because I can say honestly that I was never subject to nerves. Arsenal? Why be nervous? What happens is in your own hands. I was confident in my ability and I always did my preparation thoroughly. The more matches you play, the less you're likely to worry, though you never get blasé. When you walk out on the pitch, that is what you've been working towards all week. You're a professional. Now you're going to earn your money and to entertain the fans, who have worked hard to earn the cash to see you do your job. Even when I played for England Schoolboys in front of 93,000 people when I was only 15, I experienced no anxiety. It was just the most fantastic feeling to be walking out in that arena to do the thing which I already knew I could do better than most. I couldn't believe that anything could be so good. I was lucky with all that.

Above Come in number 11, your time is up! That's what I wanted to hear from Matt Busby, because I hated it on the left wing, hated it with a passion. During the early part of 1960/61, it was put to me by the Old Man that United faced an emergency. David Pegg had died at Munich and Albert Scanlon was leaving. He told me I was quick and two-footed, and that he wanted me to try it, so I had little choice. I used to loathe having to stand near the touchline waiting for the ball, which wasn't my natural game. I loved running and always had loads of energy, so I wanted to be in the thick of the action. Sometimes it seemed I would go 20 minutes without seeing the ball, and it drove me to distraction, though never enough to even wonder about a move away from Old Trafford. In the end I spent several years on the left flank, playing regularly for England in that position, before orthodox wingers became less common and the Old Man brought me back into central midfield. Thank the Lord! In this photograph I am not sure if I am celebrating a goal, or trying desperately to get someone to pass the ball to me.

Above It was a tumultuous afternoon in the Hillsborough mud. Football is a passionate game and when Manchester United faced Leeds in an FA Cup semi-final at the home of Sheffield Wednesday in March 1965, those hot-blooded feelings boiled over. The brawl kicked off when my brother Jack (centre) clashed with the fiery Denis Law, whose shirt is spectacularly ripped. The pair look ready for a showdown but little Bobby Collins (right), a combative character himself, is restraining Denis by the arm. As a peace-loving man, and someone not brave enough to throw a punch, I'm attempting to reason with the more tempestuously inclined Paddy Crerand, who has Leeds skipper Billy Bremner by the scruff of his neck. Meanwhile Leeds' Norman Hunter (far left) and Nobby Stiles are on the edge of the fray. Of course, there is no future in fighting on the pitch, but I can understand how people get carried away with the excitement occasionally. The game finished goalless, with Leeds winning the replay 1–0.

Opposite It's that glorious split-second of footballing truth, the moment after the ball has left your foot and has beaten the goalkeeper before hitting the net. On this occasion I'm completing my hat-trick at Ewood Park in a 5–0 victory over Blackburn in April 1965, on the run-in to our first league title since Munich. Fred Else is the custodian sailing through the air in vain pursuit of this left-foot drive from the edge of the box. The defender who didn't quite close me down is Walter Joyce, a former adversary from schoolboy football.

Opposite I was lucky in that it didn't matter which side the ball came to me, I could cope equally well with right foot or left. Here I'm hitting a cross from the left flank against Strasbourg at Old Trafford in May 1965. That evening was a bit of an anti-climax, as we had won the first leg of our Inter-Cities Fairs Cup quarter-final 5–0 in France, and the home encounter finished goalless. It was the beauty of European football back then that you didn't know much about most of your opponents before you met them. We didn't have the chance to see them on television as we do today, so often we were taking a thrilling step into the unknown.

Above OK, it wasn't hygienic, but we loved it in that communal bath. Probably a lot of people wouldn't relish the prospect of plunging in with another dozen or so sweaty, muddy bodies, but it was part of our culture, part of being a footballer. In fact, it was one of the best times of the day, getting in the water, relaxing with a beer and having a chat about the game. It was important, a bonding exercise if you like. I was appalled when they were re-designing the United dressing room and some do-gooders were saying: 'You can't jump in all together, it's not nice, it's not healthy.' But the players moaned liked hell and I'm happy to say they got their way. Seen here celebrating the 1965 league title are, left to right along the back wall, Denis Law, Nobby Stiles, Shay Brennan, Pat Dunne and Bill Foulkes. That's me by the pipe and George Best in the foreground.

Opposite I skippered Manchester United plenty of times, but I was never a natural in the role. In fact, in most cases I believe the position of captain is overrated in importance, more ceremonial than practical. There have been notable exceptions, like Billy Wright or Bobby Moore, who were inspirational natural leaders, but for the majority it is just a question of leading the team out, and maybe doing a bit of liaison between players and manager. Here I'm trotting out at Old Trafford in September 1965, followed by Irish goalkeeper Pat Dunne, who performed magnificently when we won the title in the previous term, but soon was replaced by Harry Gregg, who was returning from injury. Pat was a brilliant shot-stopper and we really appreciated the accuracy of his kicking. He was a lovely guy, too.

Above I have never known a player with as sharp a sense of anticipation as Denis Law. Whenever I took a shot he was lurking, prowling, ready to gobble up any rebound which might fall his way. The speed of his thought and his reflexes

was almost uncanny. I'd love to know what proportion of his goals came from unconsidered trifles snapped up after a 'keeper had parried somebody else's effort. In this home encounter with Fulham in April 1968 he is perfectly placed to poach yet another, but this time he wasn't needed, as my left-footed cross-shot has eluded the diving Ian Seymour and crept inside the post.

Denis Law:

Bobby, David Herd and my fellow Scot Peter Lorimer of Leeds were the three hardest strikers of a ball that I know. When Bobby or David lined up to shoot from outside the box, I always had the feeling that even if the 'keeper saved it, the ferocity of the shot might make it impossible for him to hold it. So I was always on my toes, waiting for that rebound. I didn't score every time but I was determined to be there to try and get it in the back of the net. Of course, Bobby knocked in so many unforgettable goals from outside the area, goals that I could never have scored. In fact, I am not sure if I ever got one in from that far out!

Above This is a famous shot which has done the rounds, but I have included it because I think it captures the essence of the game. The passion and the effort, the aspiration and the athleticism, they're all there.

Opposite My team-mates seemed genuinely pleased for me when I was voted Footballer of the Year in 1966, and they should have been delighted for themselves, too, because nobody ever won an award like that without having top-notch players around them. The two lads I've trusted not to drop me are

Paddy Crerand (left) and David Herd, while also pictured, left to right, are Harry Gregg, Matt Busby, Noel Cantwell, Shay Brennan, Denis Law and Nobby Stiles. Two other things strike me here: the old board which used to relay the half-time scores before the electronic era, and our raggle-taggle training kit. Trainer Jack Crompton used to pick up rugby shirts which were seconds, and therefore either free or cheap. There might have been something wrong with them all, but I liked them, because they were thick and soaked up the sweat.

Above On my way to London to collect the Footballer of the Year award. In addition to this traditional celebratory shot, the photographers wanted one of me relaxing on the train with my feet up. I was happy to comply, the pictures were duly published but then I was dumbfounded to get a letter from British Rail, admonishing me severely for putting my feet on a seat. I can't quite remember now, but I think I might have taken my shoes off anyway. I thought it was an unbelievable reaction, but I didn't lose much sleep over it!

Opposite Everybody said I'd have to make a speech when I received that coveted statuette and I did, but only a small one. It might have been a bit of an ordeal in front of so many great football men – my heroes Stanley Matthews and Tom Finney were there – and all those journalists, but by the time I got to my feet lots of people had come over to congratulate me, which had set me at my ease.

Above Though we're both looking a wee bit preoccupied ahead of the action, it was a pleasure to greet my pal Eusebio, a delightfully unassuming character, when Benfica came to Old Trafford for the first leg of our European Cup quarter-final in February 1966. He was one of the top players in the world at the time, and Lisbon's mighty Eagles, who had already lifted the trophy twice and were the previous year's beaten finalists, were among the toughest opposition imaginable. We won 3–2 that night but there was a widespread feeling that probably we had not quite done enough to progress. Certainly we expected a hard slog in Portugal in five weeks' time . . .

Above Facing Benfica at the Stadium of Light, where they had never been beaten in European competition, might have been an intimidating business. Instead it turned out to be the finest United performance of my career, a night on which everything clicked perfectly. It has passed into folklore that Matt told us to keep it steady for 20 minutes, but that George hadn't paid particular attention. So he struck twice in the first 12 minutes, we were three up at the break and won 5–1. We had just never stopped going forward; we felt superhuman. The pitch was flooded with fans, and I was euphoric as I came off. Even the Portuguese felt they'd just witnessed something special.

Left Enjoying a beer in the dressing room after the match are the four scorers, left to right, John Connelly, Paddy Crerand, George Best and myself. John was a tough lad for a winger, very talented and extremely underrated. I think he can be forgiven for naming his fish-and-chip shop Connelly's Plaice!

Left The Old Trafford sun glints off the Ballon d'Or, which I had received after being voted European Footballer of the Year for 1966. I was overjoyed by the award, naturally, but news of it arrived on a bad day. I was with the lads and we heard it on the radio ahead of a meeting with Sheffield United. I had a lousy game, we lost and I felt dreadful. If I could have swapped that award for a point that day, then I'd have done it.

Below Even in the extravagantly rich history of Manchester United, this is a unique moment. There on the Old Trafford pitch are three European Footballers of the Year from our club, along with Matt Busby, which was appropriate because it was his vision and drive to get United into Europe which enabled Denis Law, myself and George Best to attain these heights. Journalist Max Urbini (left) of *France Football* has just presented the 1968 award to George. I don't know why I'm besuited; I must have been sidelined with a knock.

Denis Law:

Bobby Charlton is in the very highest category of footballers there have ever been. At that level you can talk about Stanley Matthews and the great Tom Finney, then there was Jimmy Greaves and George Best, all players with something you haven't seen before. Bobby is on a par with them, and he would always be up there with the top men from any era. It was wonderful to play with him. He made it so easy. For instance, he was one of the finest crossers of a ball I ever encountered, equally superb with left foot and right. And apart from all his wonderful skills, Bobby was a grafter. He was up and down the pitch all the time: he never stopped running. He was a fantastic athlete.

Above Taking to the air to launch a left-foot effort at Chelsea, despite the close attentions of Eddie McCreadie, their world-class Scottish international left back. I know it didn't go in because I never scored at Stamford Bridge during the middle and late 1960s, yet I always enjoyed playing there. The surroundings were familiar because sometimes I trained at the Bridge if I had played for England on a Wednesday and United were in London on the following Saturday. I didn't do my work with the Chelsea team, instead going in during the afternoon when their players had usually gone home. But on one occasion I was in the bathroom as their defender Dave Webb walked past the open doorway. The next minute I heard his puzzled voice telling some team-mates: 'I've just looked in the bathroom, and there's a bloke in there who's the spitting image of Bobby Charlton!'

Opposite Was Bobby Moore the type of man to try and psych out an opponent ahead of a vital game? Absolutely not. Thus when we travelled to Upton Park on 6 May 1967, needing to beat West Ham to clinch the league championship, our exchanges at kick-off could not have been more straightforward. He was a true sportsman, one of the most dignified figures in the game and, of course, he was my pal from our England experiences together. As it turned out, it was our day. I put us ahead after two minutes, we were three up in ten and we ran out 6–1 winners. Upton Park was not an easy place to go to, the springtime pitch was hard and bouncy, and the Hammers were a decent footballing side, but we were so motivated by the prize dangling before us that we simply trounced them.

Above Bobby Moore wasn't particularly fast, or powerful in the air, or more skilful than the next man. But he saw everything, read the game with remarkable certainty, and was adept at snuffing out danger as he has here, sliding in ahead of me to nick the ball to safety.

Right Paddy Crerand climbs beyond me to head our second goal at West Ham and put us well on the way to our second title in three years. Paddy didn't score too many and he was never

going to be a sprint champion, but he was a glorious user of the ball, particularly over long distances, and I think the pair of us complemented each other in midfield. A proud, garrulous and sometimes boisterous Scot, he was not one to shrink from expressing his opinions in the dressing room . . . or anywhere else, for that matter!

Above There are few places more joyous than a football dressing room after a trophy has been secured; and there is nothing more calculated to foster team spirit than the feeling of having lifted a prize by striving shoulder to shoulder, on good days and bad, over the course of a whole season. This was the scene at Upton Park after our demolition of West Ham, which had confirmed us as champions. A special word here for Tony Dunne, fourth from the right at the front. Because he was a lovely modest chap, sometimes the cheerful Irishman is forgotten when the bouquets are handed out, but it ought to be said that for a considerable period he was the best left back in Europe. He was so quick and intelligent, and I had the pleasure of working closely with him when we were defending our left flank. Tony is an unsung hero who played a crucial part in so many United triumphs. Raising their glasses here are, left to right, front row: Denis Law, Johnny Aston, Shay Brennan, Bill Foulkes, Tony, Paddy Crerand, Nobby Stiles and myself. At the back are close pals David Sadler and George Best, while Alex Stepney is out of shot.

Above Sitting next to George Best at the right end of the front row of United's 1966/67 championship line-up is one of the unluckiest young players I have known. His name is Bobby Noble and he was a ruthlessly flinty young full back with the footballing world at his feet, having forced his way into this team by dint of sheer ability and application when only just out of his teens. But then he was seriously injured in a car accident and never played again, bringing home to every one of us just how lucky we were. I was proud to be part of this side, which won nearly everything it went for and was as good as any I ever played in, including the pre-Munich combination. Back row, left to right: Noel Cantwell, David Sadler, David Herd, Bill Foulkes, Jimmy Ryan, Jack Crompton (trainer). Middle: David Gaskell, Shay Brennan, myself, Johnny Aston, Paddy Crerand, Alex Stepney. Front: John Fitzpatrick, Nobby Stiles, Tony Dunne, Matt Busby (manager), Denis Law, George Best, Bobby Noble.

Opposite Anyone who thinks it's easy being a professional footballer should take a look at Denis Law and myself, so absolutely knackered we can hardly move at the end of a pre-season stamina session in the little gym under the south stand at Old Trafford. I detested that annual slog, not only because it was so hard to get my body working after the summer break, but also because there was no end-product in the form of a game. Basically we were running in July so we'd be able to keep running in March and April. It made sense, we knew we needed it, but God how it hurt! Jack Crompton was in charge and he was a hard taskmaster. I don't think everybody believed in his old-school programmes, though I still do some of them now. My back can get stiff just leaning on the stool at the breakfast table. That's when I lie on the kitchen floor and do some of Jack's exercises together with modern routines given to me by my daughter Andrea, who's a physiotherapist.

Above I didn't always celebrate my goals as extravagantly as this, but it *was* against Manchester City, and there was always a special tingle when I scored against them. Jimmy Murphy wound us up about City, dinned into us that it meant more than an ordinary game, that our fans needed us to win so they could hold their heads high at work on Monday morning. I hadn't come from Manchester so I hadn't experienced that particular rivalry. I supported Newcastle as a little lad, not United or City, but I soon picked up on the partisan feeling. I enjoyed playing at Maine Road, which had a decent pitch and an excellent atmosphere, and I relished it particularly on this occasion in September 1967 as I hit the target twice in a 2–1 victory. I'd guess Ken Mulhearn, the beaten goalkeeper, would not have shared my feelings.

Above There are certain goals I'll always remember and this was one of them. It was April 1968, we were in a decent position as we attempted to defend our league title, but with only three minutes left of the first half at Southampton, we were trailing to strikes by Terry Paine and Ron Davies. Then Francis Burns broke down the left to reach the dead-ball line and I sprinted forward to support him, just as Jimmy Murphy had always taught me. Our adventurous overlapper pulled the ball back to the edge of the six-yard box and I nipped between Hughie Fisher (left) and Jimmy

Gabriel to meet it, but as it reached me it bounced much too high for a straightforward shot. What followed was pure instinct. It was a question of getting my balance and finding a way of keeping the ball down. I met it on the full volley, concentrating fiercely on getting over the ball, and it just flew past 'keeper Eric Martin into the net. I was quite pleased with that because I'd managed to anticipate the flight and made the right decision. Two minutes later I was even happier as George Best had equalised, but unfortunately we were unable to force a winner.

Above Look at that sea of faces behind me as I take this corner at Old Trafford. They all seem to me as if they're thinking: 'I wish *I* was a footballer.' It's not that they're in awe of me in the slightest; it could be anybody kicking the ball. It's just that their love of the game is so transparent. I always felt responsible for these people, all living their individual lives, yet all united for an hour and a half in something they love. Marvellous!

Right The Big Four, a tag applied by ourselves with pronounced irony and which referred to the card school maintained by myself along with, left to right, David Herd, Shay Brennan and Nobby Stiles. We were close pals and we played together on buses, trains and planes on the constant journeys we were making throughout the 1960s. Who was the sharpest? Well, I think I was all right; Nobby would say the same of himself and Shay was good, but somehow David just couldn't help letting you know what was in his hand. He would never have made his fortune as a gambler. Mind, we only played for pennies, usually at cribbage. We were vastly differing characters, but somehow we just gelled. David was a smart lad and a really tremendous goal-scorer with a cannonball shot. Sometimes he would shatter the picket fence which used to surround Old Trafford, often when merely kicking in before the game. I was afraid that one day he would decapitate somebody in the crowd. Shay was the funny lad, a sunny charmer from an Irish family who liked the dogs, but never so much as turned a hair if he lost a bet. His outlook on life was unbelievably laid back and I never met a more popular individual. As for Nobby, he was the friendly, open-hearted local boy renowned for his clumsiness, which we laughed at but never in a nasty way. We were a terrific little group and we had great times, great times.

Opposite Bill Foulkes and I warm our freezing hands in front of a blazing open fire at my favourite hotel in the whole world. It's the County Hotel in Durham, and we used it when we were away to Newcastle or Sunderland. It's very old and in the 1960s it had no central heating, so you got into bed with an old-fashioned hot-water bottle. The food was fantastic and we all loved it there. Actually it's quite a famous place in the North East, and prime minister Harold Wilson used to stand on its balcony to take salutes at the annual miners' picnics. On this occasion it was the night before we played at St James' Park in December 1967. We drew two-apiece.

Bill Foulkes:

Bobby Charlton was some footballer and he was some man. He was the one we could always look to when we needed something special, the one the fans always expected to score a goal, and the one our opponents feared because they knew he could hurt them. When Bobby took possession there was always a special buzz around the ground as though something dramatic was going to happen, and so often it did.

Not only that, but he could make the game look beautiful, too. I reckon Pelé must have been thinking of Bobby when he coined his famous phrase. For a footballer, he offered an unparalleled combination of grace, power and precision. It added up to greatness and something more, something I can only call beauty. He could make the difference. It was almost like playing alongside Roy of the Rovers. Well, three of them actually, because there was Denis Law and George Best, too.

But for all his fabulous talent, there was never any side to Bobby. He was always modest, always unassuming, always down-to-earth, the perfect example for any young lad watching the game from the terraces or for any young professional on his way up at the club.

I think he and I always shared a special bond because we both came from coal-mining backgrounds, and then later we had the accident at Munich in common, too.

CHAPTER 6

The unique conquest

Left 'Have you heard Alf's latest? He reckons England will win the World Cup!' We can be cavalier about it now, but actually my pal Ray Wilson and I would never have been taking the mick out of the England manager's prediction. What Alf Ramsey said in the England camp was law, and if he said we were going to win the World Cup, who were we to argue? Meanwhile whatever Ray was really saying made me laugh and pull a face, but if trainer Harold Shepherdson heard it, he was not amused. Ray and I roomed together and became very close. He was a fantastic man, a bit of a leader who would never be intimidated, but with a dry sense of humour. Oh, yes, and he was the best left back in the world.

Right Time can drag for footballers between matches in a lengthy tournament, so Alf Ramsey made sure there was plenty of enjoyable but undemanding activities on offer while we were together for the 1966 World Cup finals. There were a few games of cricket, nothing too strenuous, nothing too expert and nothing too serious. Certainly Jack and I don't appear to be under immense strain as we await our turn to bat, and my bowling was never going to take any wickets. I think I was more concerned with not looking too ridiculous than ensuring that the ball was on the wicket.

Below Leaning on the ropes at a London boxing gym are Bobby Moore (standing) and, left to right, my brother Jack, Ray Wilson, Jimmy Greaves and myself. Muhammad Ali was in town and we had hoped to see him in action, but we had to leave for our own training before he arrived. Jimmy seems happy enough at this point, but understandably his mood deteriorated when he wasn't picked for the final against West Germany. That must have been a tough decision for Alf, but he never shrunk from those.

Opposite Golf tends to be a favourite with lots of footballers, and I quite enjoyed it but was never in danger of getting addicted. Jack looks to be satisfied with his shot, but I have to admit there's a hint of frustration on my face . . .

Roger Hunt:

It's characteristically generous of Bobby to mention my efforts in contributing to his goal, but really I was just doing my job as a front-runner and the plaudits should be directed towards his spectacular strike. The ball was a long, long way from goal when I gave it to him, so he had more than a bit to do. It was a crucial moment in our campaign because the press had slated us mercilessly after the Uruguay match and this lifted a weight from our shoulders. It was a pleasure to play alongside such a brilliant performer as Bobby and I always got on well with him off the field, too. We gelled right from the beginning and he's been a really good friend down the years.

Left It was the goal which got our World Cup up and running, and one for which I seem to be remembered, but the fact is that so much of the credit for it should go to Roger Hunt. After a frustrating goalless draw with Uruguay, we were a little over half an hour into the second group game, against Mexico at Wembley, with nothing on the board. Then Roger gave me the ball inside our half and set off running, taking several defenders with him. I moved forward and when the space opened up in front of me, I followed Jimmy Murphy's advice to keep advancing. Nobody came to me and when I was about 30 yards out, I just hit it towards the rectangle with my right foot. It was the product of more Murphy wisdom: 'Don't place it, let the 'keeper wonder where it's going. If you don't know then how can he?' It flew so sweetly and a lot of tension was released. We were on our way. But if Roger hadn't been so typically selfless I'd have had to lay the ball off and we'd have taken another route. Who knows what might have happened?

Below When a pressman handed me this sombrero after we had beaten Mexico, I thought: 'Why not?' I wouldn't have done anything that made me look *too* stupid, but we were all happy at getting back on track, and when you're happy you do daft things. At least Norman Hunter thought it was funny!

Above If this is how the winners look, how must the losers be feeling? Jimmy Greaves (centre), Martin Peters and I are lost in thought as we leave the Wembley pitch after beating France 2–0, courtesy of a brace of goals from Roger Hunt, to qualify for the quarter-finals of the World Cup. I was reflecting that it hadn't been a great game or a stirring victory, and I was a little worried that my pal Nobby might have landed himself in hot water over what I am sure was no more than a mistimed tackle on Jacques Simon. As for Jimmy, he was nursing a gashed shin that would need 14 stitches. If he was fearing at that moment that his World Cup was over, then he was right.

Opposite top There was a high, bright sun. The Wembley shadows were pin-sharp. It was a fine day for a quarter-final showdown – and, by my reckoning, Argentina were the hardest team we would be asked to face, even if we went all the way. So it proved. They were a fantastically accomplished all-round side but, sadly for them, they failed utterly to do themselves justice as footballers. There's something that pushes them over the edge sometimes, as when their skipper Antonio Rattin was manhandling the referee, who had no alternative but to send him off. Ironically, I'm a very big pal of his these days, and he tells me that sort of behaviour is acceptable in Argentina. Crazy! As for the single goal that beat them, it was unstoppable. Martin Peters' outswinging cross was met by Geoff Hurst's glancing header on the run, and after that we knew we'd done it. In this shot, taken early in the game, I'm attempting to accelerate away from their defender Roberto Ferreiro. He didn't catch me but the move came to nothing.

Right After the final whistle Alf Ramsey was livid about the Argentinians' behaviour and prevented George Cohen from swapping his shirt. I could understand why, but I didn't mind handing mine over. We'd won the game; they could have the shirt.

Above Just as I owed a huge debt to Roger Hunt for my goal against Mexico, so Geoff Hurst deserved a mountain of praise for setting up my second strike against Portugal in the semi-final. We were one up with ten minutes left when the ball went into their box. Geoff got hold of it and protected it brilliantly as he looked up to see me charging forward from midfield. I was praying he wouldn't lay it to me early or I would have been too far out, but his timing was perfect as he rolled it into my path as I reached the edge of the area. I couldn't do anything else but whack it hard and low and it fizzed just inside the far post. Lovely!

It was in marked contrast to my earlier goal, which actually gave me even more satisfaction. A loose ball reached me about 18 yards out and, with the net gaping, I threaded it between a confusion of bodies. I didn't hit it too hard but trusted that beautifully true pitch and literally passed it between the posts. It would have been easy to blaze it over the bar, so I was pleased that I kept my cool.

Above The final whistle has gone, we have beaten Portugal 2–1, Jack is arriving to enfold me in a bear hug and sweet realisation is just dawning that we are in the final of the World Cup. My feeling was that there was no way we would lose now, having come so far. Honestly, I didn't contemplate defeat for even a single moment.

Right Suddenly, after the shenanigans indulged in by Argentina in the previous match, our semi-final meeting with Portugal demonstrated that football could, indeed, be a truly beautiful game. Both sides entertained royally and the game was played in a wonderful spirit, as exemplified by Eusebio. When it was over and he congratulated me, taking my face in both his hands, I felt sorry for him because I knew how much this World Cup had meant to him and his country. There was, and there will always remain, a heartfelt respect between the two of us. Eusebio was one of the greatest players I ever faced and a true sportsman.

anyone else to shadow because I did have a good engine and I had never felt so well. As it turned out, the mere fact that I was close to him meant that his team-mates barely gave him the ball, so Alf got it right. Towards the end of the game both Franz and I looked shattered, and we were. He told me later that it was the most tired he had been in his life.

Left Exhausted though I felt, there was still the energy to make a point to the Swiss referee Gottfried Dienst. I can't be certain, but from the copious amounts of sweat and the pained expression, probably this was during the excruciatingly tense prelude to the fateful free-kick awarded shortly before the end of normal time, with England leading 2–1.

Opposite Franz Beckenbauer and myself might have been a pair of Siamese twins, so close did we stick to each other in the World Cup final. Alf made the decision that this precociously and comprehensively gifted young German was the only man on their side who could do us real damage if he was given the freedom of the pitch, so he detailed me to be his warder. Ironically, the German camp had given Franz the job of looking after me, so, to a large degree, we cancelled each other out. I wasn't a tackler or a marker by trade so I couldn't play my natural game, but that didn't bother me. It was enough to be there and doing something important for the team. I wouldn't have wanted to give him to

Below People look at me blankly when I mention it because everyone recalls the day of the World Cup final as scorching hot, but there was actually a heavy summer shower which might have had a profound effect on the outcome of the game. It was fairly late on in proceedings when the ball fizzed across the box just within my reach. Because of how it was spinning it wasn't a great opportunity, but I had a quick flash at it, only to fluff it badly and the ball finished well wide. The turf had become saturated, almost as slippery as glass, and I lost my balance at precisely the wrong moment. It could have been the winner, but in the end it didn't matter.

Above The controversy still rages more than four decades on, but I am adamant that when Geoff Hurst's injury-time shot struck the crossbar and bounced down, it crossed the line before spinning back into play. I saw it happen with my own eyes and so did Roger Hunt, one of the straightest men in football, who turned to celebrate rather than knocking in the rebound as he could easily have done. For a split-second I was overjoyed, but then out of the corner of my eye I spotted that the linesman had raised his flag, and I was afraid he'd disallowed it.

Opposite Suddenly I was aghast at what I perceived to be flagrant injustice. Some of the Germans were moaning – though not, significantly, either Franz Beckenbauer (left) or Wolfgang Overath (second right) who were both well placed – and I'm shouting, 'You can't moan. It went over the line!' After an agonising chat between referee Gottfried Dienst and linesman Tofik Bakhramov, the goal was given and we were 3–2 to the good. I still get quizzed on this every time I go to Germany, but Franz always admits graciously that we were the best team with the greater hunger to win.

Above When the final whistle went, I must have been farther from Franz Beckenbauer (left) than I had been all afternoon. The crowd behind the goal were going crazy and, in what felt to me like a moment of profound union, I raised my arms to celebrate with them. The record books state that there were 96,924 people in the ground, and I reckon I must have spoken to every one of them, plus a few more!

Opposite An instant or two after the signal that our quest was over, I found myself on my knees, folded in the arms of my brother. There was no deep exchange of words. He said: 'Well, what about that, Kiddo?' I think it crossed my mind that our lives would never be the same again, but I don't remember if I gave voice to the thought. We didn't seek each other out; we just bumped into one another, then we were enveloped in a cacophony of sound the like of which I'd never heard. England had never really gone close to winning the World Cup, and now we had done it. It's a moment that will live with me forever. In its intensity it was almost religious.

Jack Charlton:

I was on my knees at the end because I'd chased Geoff Hurst about 400 yards round the pitch, trying to catch him when he'd completed his hat-trick. In the end I caught up with him and I gave him a hug, and I gave Our Kid a hug and I gave everybody a hug. By then I was knackered and I collapsed on my knees. I don't know whether I said a prayer. I probably did. Bobby was emotional and couldn't say much, only something like: 'What have we got to win now?'

Left In our moment of supreme triumph, the other lads are smiling like they'll never stop, but even as I brandish aloft the precious Jules Rimet trophy, for which we had laboured so long and so hard, my face is wracked with deep emotion. It looks as though I'm close to tears and, if I'm honest, that's the way it was. People are different. This time was just as magical to me as to the others, but I just choked up. It's always like that with me. I get moved beyond measure watching people from any field achieve something when they have worked for it, made sacrifices for it, like maybe a young girl who has sailed round the world or a swimmer who has got up at 4.30 in the morning for three years just to train. Such obscure considerations were, I'm sure, a long way from the thoughts of, left to right, Gordon Banks, Ray Wilson, Alan Ball (who looks to be comforting me), Bobby Moore and George Cohen.

Below Champagne, Bobby? No thanks, make mine a beer. I've never been a great one for the bubbly, even after the World Cup final. We sat in a room with the other three semi-finalists, the West Germans, the Portuguese and the Russians. While we were there, someone presented all the England lads with the cloth for a bespoke suit. Uwe Seeler, the German captain, was looking a little glum so I gave mine to him.

Right This is my dad, calling for a toast with the WAGs – of course, they didn't call them that in 1966 – after the World Cup final. That's the smartest I ever saw him dressed, and certainly it's the only time I knew him to stand up like that in company. But I suppose it was a bit of a special occasion, having two sons help to win the World Cup! Like my wife Norma, in front of him to his left, he looks so proud and happy. Dad actually missed the semi-final because he didn't want somebody else to have to do his shift at the pit back in Ashington, but he was talked into coming to the final. I guess it seems strange compared to modern custom, but the families weren't invited to eat with the players, who were celebrating in a separate room.

Below A tender moment among the pandemonium at a crowded hotel – the lifts had long since packed up – as Norma and I meet for the first time since I had become a World Cup winner. This was after we had eaten and a little before we went out for the evening with Bobby Moore, Ray Wilson, George Eastham and their wives to the Playboy Club.

Above All spruced up and with not a tear in sight, the victorious England team, complete with the gleaming golden prize, face the camera for the official picture in the grounds of our hotel, which was quite unusual in that Alf always fostered the ethos of the squad. This is just the 11 players who turned out on the big day, along with the manager and trainer. It was a moment of supreme satisfaction because our achievement will stand forever. We can say we were the best in the world, and nobody can argue. Back row, left to right: Harold Shepherdson, Nobby Stiles, Roger Hunt, Gordon Banks, Jack Charlton, George Cohen, Ray Wilson, Alf Ramsey. Front: Martin Peters, Geoff Hurst, Bobby Moore, Alan Ball, myself.

Above Riding in a yellow Rolls-Royce, Jack and I make an unforgettable journey of about a mile from our family home in Beatrice Street to Ashington town hall for a reception to honour our World Cup victory. It was an almost surreal experience to return to the little back streets, where we had been raised and knew every brick, as world champions. We were presented with beautiful Omega watches, and then there was a function at which it felt like I shook every hand in the North East. The other England lads would have been treated similarly in their home towns; I just felt so incredibly proud to be experiencing this with my brother. All the flags and bunting came out, people danced and waved in the street; it was just like when the war ended or the coronation of the Queen. In many people's eyes it *was* like winning the war, and not just because our opponents had been Germany. It was the fact that it gave the whole community something to celebrate.

Below Nearly three months on from Wembley and the World Cup winners are reunited at Windsor Park, Belfast. We had been lauded all summer, which had been magical, but it made our future matches more difficult because everybody wanted to beat us, to knock us off our perch. However, with Alf Ramsey still at the helm, there was never going to be any resting on our laurels, and we beat Northern Ireland 2–0.

CHAPTER 7

Our Holy Grail

Above I must have been photographed millions of times down the years, yet of all the countless images that I have seen, this is my favourite. It is a moment in the dressing room at the Bernabeu Stadium in May 1968 after we had come from 3–1 behind on the night, back from the dead really, to draw 3–3 with Real Madrid in the semi-final of the European Cup and go through to the final, thanks to our 1–0 victory at Old Trafford three weeks earlier. It was a moment of both sublime

satisfaction and overwhelming emotion as my thoughts flickered back inevitably to the lads who couldn't be with us, but who had given so much to the cause of Manchester United. When Matt Busby grabbed me for a cuddle, the thought occurred that I was dripping with sweat, but that was hardly going to bother the Old Man when he had moved so close to the ultimate prize he had craved for so long. The European crown has often been described as his equivalent of the Holy Grail, and I'd say that

Below When the semi-final ended in Madrid, and we had won on aggregate, I was in a state of collapse, emotional as much as physical, although I'm certain in retrospect that I was badly dehydrated. No one thought about that in those days. There were hordes of fans on the pitch, people were milling around me and shouting, and I'm not ashamed to say I felt totally drained. The whole long journey that we had made in Europe seemed to flash before my eyes. I had been desperate to reach that final, and nagging away at the back of my mind had been the thought that maybe this was our last chance. I lay flat on my back for a minute or so, trying to take it all in, how we had been reprieved from the brink of elimination. This time, maybe, fate was on our side. Eventually I was helped to my feet by two fans and young Brian Kidd, and I went off to join the celebrations. I had never been so happy in my life.

was right. It was important to me, too, to share the joy with Jimmy Murphy (left), unquestionably the premier influence on my development as a player, and one of the warmest, most genuine football men I have ever known. I always had vast affection, too, for the figure on the right, Jack Crompton, our faithful, hard-working trainer and another lovely man with United in his heart.

Right After all United had been through, I couldn't envisage any set of circumstances in which we would lose the final. With every fibre of my being I believed we would reach out and claim our ultimate prize. But still it would have been fatal to our chances if we had underestimated Benfica. Although they didn't have a great record against us, they were battle-hardened and successful in Europe, and in Mario Coluna they had a born leader. We had faced each other plenty of times for both club and country and we were pals. Now, as we exchanged pennants before kick-off, I could sense the determination in Mario that, having lost their last two finals, they were desperate to be European champions again.

Below With the massed ranks of the Benfica rearguard lining up in front of me to repel this first-half free-kick, I opted for a little trickery. The Portuguese had some solid lads in their wall, including Eusebio (number 10), and I couldn't see much of the goal as I ran up to the ball. So it was time for Plan B. Instead of having a crack, I chipped a little pass to Brian Kidd, whose job it was to lay the ball into space behind the barrier so that I or one of the other lads might nip through on the 'keeper. Moves like that look fantastic when they work, but this one didn't. Worth a try, though.

Above I've opened the scoring eight minutes into the second half of the European Cup final with what looked like a perfect glancing header, but to be perfectly honest there was a little bit of luck involved. I was never brilliant in the air – not so bad, perhaps, if I had plenty of time and space, but otherwise nothing special – so when the ball went out to David Sadler on the left, I ran to the near post to act as a decoy for the lads who could head it. David knocked it in with a little bit of spin and, with the goal behind me, I just helped it on with a faint touch. The next thing I knew, glory of glories, it had dropped just inside the far post. The 'keeper, Jose Henrique, never had a chance, yet I'd had no idea of aiming for the goal. It was almost as if, on this night of destiny for Manchester United, the ball had been guided on its path by some unseen celestial hand. I've barely landed from my leap and Brian Kidd is already celebrating. After missing one or two decent chances, we were on our way.

David Sadler:

I had drifted out to the left wing, and I wasn't the type who was going to dash for the byline. I sensed Bobby making a run somewhere around the near post, so I turned back and curled in a cross with my right foot. Sometimes you pick someone out deliberately but on the vast majority of occasions it's not that clear cut. You put the ball into a danger area and hope something comes of it. That's the reality of football and that's what happened here. When it dropped in the net it looked as though it had been planned meticulously, but I assure you it hadn't. People do play the odds. There's a fair bit of hit-and-hope, even at the top level. Of course, when the ball reached Bobby there was still a lot for him to do, but in his case it never surprised anyone when he came up trumps because he was a world-class operator, one of the greatest footballers there has ever been. To say it was a pleasure to play alongside him is putting it mildly.

Above By the time this one went in to make it 4–1, Benfica had stunned us with Graca's equaliser, then given us an almighty scare when Eusebio was through on goal, spearing the tortured thought 'This *cannot* be!' across my mind. Mercifully he opted for a spectacular rather than a clinical finish and was thwarted by an instinctive save from our 'keeper Alex Stepney. The Portuguese looked shattered during the break before extra time, and soon goals from George Best and Brian Kidd made the game safe. Then Brian went down the right and once again I sprinted instinctively to the near post to pull defenders out of the way. But he found me with his cross, I turned it on with my right foot and it floated beyond the reach of Henrique for our third goal in seven minutes. Everything else was like a visit to paradise. Benfica's gallant challenge was broken and we strolled through the final quarter of the game as if we were on cloud nine.

Above and opposite In the act of scoring the fourth goal, I had run off the pitch and am just returning as George arrives like an express train to hurl himself into my arms. With the Wembley crowd going berserk and the emotion rolling down from the stands, it is an immaculate moment, a consummation of everything we had dreamed, separately but ultimately with a single thread, that football could deliver. I was tired, weary to my bones, but still there was strength to sweep the little Irish genius from his feet, those feet that had danced so dazzlingly to create the goal which had brought Benfica to their knees. We knew in that fleeting but precious interlude that the European Cup was destined for Manchester, that Matt Busby's long and gruelling quest was only 20 minutes away from the perfect conclusion.

Two contrasting faces of my pal Nobby Stiles, one of the most genuine and sometimes criminally underrated footballers who ever walked on to a pitch. On the right he is in warrior mode, his front teeth tucked away safely in the dressing room, not long after the final whistle had blown on the most joyous night of our Manchester United careers. What a victory he is saluting! All of us, and especially a Mancunian born and bred like Nobby, were acutely aware of the extra significance of our achievement in securing the prize Matt Busby cherished above all others, in the light of the 23 lives lost at Munich ten years earlier as United had appeared then to be closing in on European glory. It had been a sultry night at Wembley – just look at the sweat on our shirts – and I was dehydrated, with barely energy left to speak. Nobby, though, was still full of beans, if not wholly coherent, as he slobbered at me something along the lines of, 'We've done it, Bob. It had to be done, and we've done it at last!' He was right, and it flashed across my mind that his contribution had been colossal, not only policing the great Eusebio but anticipating danger wherever it might occur. Nobby was a superb reader of the game, brilliant at sniffing out danger, and he remains one of my closest friends, which is why I thought I'd better include a shot of him at his most handsome, with dentures firmly inserted.

Nobby Stiles:

Bobby and I have always been close. When my brother-in-law Johnny Giles went to Leeds in 1963, I felt a little bit isolated, a little bit lost, particularly when Matt Busby used to take us on training breaks to the Norbreck Hotel in Blackpool. I could have been on my own, but Bobby and Shay Brennan were brilliant, they took me under their wing and we became firm friends. They were the ones who had time for me, the ones with that niceness about them. They helped to give me confidence in myself and I always felt I owed a lot to the pair of them.

Besides being a great player, blessed with superb balance and grace, and with power and control in either foot, Bobby is a lovely man. People who don't know him sometimes misjudge him. They think he is usually serious, but that's not so. He's got this lovely dry sense of humour that I find quite hilarious at times.

I played behind him for both United and England. I was told my job was to win the ball, then give it to Bobby. He could win any game for you, out of nothing. He would never hide from the ball, even when things weren't going well. He always wanted it, always wanted to help you out, and that takes a special kind of courage.

Above When Italian referee Concetto Lo Bello raised the whistle to his lips for the final time, Matt Busby was engulfed and pandemonium reigned. Everybody was pulling and pushing and hugging and back-slapping. The gathering dusk of that balmy Wembley evening was split by the flashes of what seemed like a thousand cameras. It was enough to faze anyone, let alone a man who had been through so much, given so unsparingly of himself for so long. I almost felt the need to check he was all right, but seeing his wide grin I held back until the hectic activity around the Old Man had calmed down a bit. Eventually I reached him and gave him a long hug. There was absolutely no need for words. It had been his pioneering team that had been devastated on the European trail, and this was their symbolic rebirth. Tears were shed and nothing could bring back the lives that had been lost, but here, at least, was some sort of balance, perhaps even a degree of closure. Somehow Munich would have had a different significance for Manchester United if we hadn't won at Wembley on that tumultuous night in May 1968.

Right Brian Kidd, the Collyhurst lad whose goal on his 19th birthday had helped to secure for Matt Busby his heart's desire, drapes an arm around the Old Man in congratulation. Paddy Crerand (left), the exuberant Scottish wing half who had performed so magnificently, supplementing his customary creativity with a lung-searing shift of box-to-box toil in the sultry conditions, weighs in with another cuddle.

Above I have untold affection for Bill Foulkes. We'd been through so much together, and we were the sole survivors of the accident at Munich who went out to meet Benfica at Wembley. So when the game was over, he was the first man I sought out. We exchanged some words, and although they have gone from my head after more than 40 years, I know they were deeply emotional. Bill was renowned for being hard – the way he mastered the giant Jose Torres during the game was a telling illustration of that – and for being dour, but that didn't mean he had no finer feelings. When I walked off that pitch after beating Benfica, I was proud to have him at my side.

Above Look at that sweat – it's a wonder I had the strength left to lift the European Cup. Next to me Alex Stepney might be gazing at his reflection in that lovely gigantic chunk of silverware, while behind him Bill Foulkes is belying his reputation for sternness, his face lit up like a little boy in a sweetshop. In the bottom right-hand corner is Nobby Stiles who, like me, had to miss the following day's reception at Manchester town hall because we had to join up with the England party ahead of the European Nations Cup. Not surprisingly, I suppose, I'm fond of this picture and I've got about 3,000 copies of it. When I returned to Old Trafford as a director, then began travelling and doing PR, it was felt I needed a photo to hand out, and I thought this would be something people might remember.

Above How marvellous it was to share the most cherished achievement of my Manchester United career with one of my closest pals, Shay Brennan (left). Shay was a bubbly character and he relished the notion that he had made our second, and match-turning, goal for George Best. Actually, his contribution was a back-pass to 'keeper Alex Stepney, here seen grinning behind me, whose towering drop-kick fell into the path of the boy from Belfast. That left George with the small matter of dribbling past two opponents before putting the ball in the net, but he was a generous lad and never begrudged Shay his share of the glory! That night, I'm sure, Shay would have enjoyed the celebration party, but I can't report at first hand because I missed it. I was dehydrated after the match, had a couple of beers because I was unbelievably thirsty, then got back to the hotel and fainted. I tried about four times to get out of the room, but in the end Norma had to go down without me. So I missed Matt singing 'What a Wonderful World', but I couldn't help it. I was completely flaked out.

CHAPTER 8

What might have been

Opposite I never stop saying this to myself, but what a lucky man I was the day I married Norma. She enjoys travelling and meeting people from all walks of life, and there is *nowhere* I can't take her with total confidence that she will fit in and chat to whoever is around. If I have to leave her for a few minutes, then every time I come back she's made new friends. If it's football people, then Norma's especially brilliant. She likes the game enough to talk about it knowledgeably, though she doesn't get dogmatic or opinionated about it. Everybody thinks the world of her and if she happens not to be with me when I visit a ground, then invariably people ask after her and urge me to make sure she accompanies me the next time. Norma's fantastic and I could never have managed without her.

Above Prime Minister Harold Wilson always liked to give the impression that he was a football fan, and he would talk about Halifax, Bradford and his own team, Huddersfield, but I'm not too sure how much of a sage he was on the subject. Of course, he was a politician, so he knew how to gloss over areas he didn't know too much about. Norma and I were at Number 10 for a thank-you reception in the wake of England's World Cup triumph, and Mr Wilson would joke that he should take the credit. He never missed a chance to say that we won the World Cup because there was a Labour government. It's fairer to say that our victory represented a huge plus for this country politically, and in terms of trade. A win like that could do far more for England's prestige than any number of speeches.

It was an awesome feeling, running across the huge empty bowl of Wembley Stadium, with hardly another soul in sight. The precise occasion escapes me, but I believe I was testing out an injured ankle ahead of an international against Sweden in the spring of 1968. Wasn't Wembley beautiful? People called it an outmoded concrete monstrosity, but it was steeped in history and it had an atmosphere all its own. People loved the twin towers, and it was sad that they couldn't be retained, but they disintegrated when they were taken down during the redevelopment. Best of all, though, was the pitch. If people thought Wembley was a great place to watch football, it was a better place to play. The ball ran so true; you could put your life on it. Of course, that was before they used it for the Horse of the Year Show – what a catastrophe that was. It left all the drains broken and suddenly we were playing on mud, with divots coming up all over the place. People talked about the hallowed turf, and that's how it should have been, but in the end it was anything but.

Left I was not a great lover of man-to-man marking. I couldn't understand why anyone would want to run around all match without having much of a kick at the ball, and that was my feeling despite being detailed to do just that against Franz Beckenbauer in the World Cup final. I knew it was for the good of the team so I was happy to do it, but from a personal point of view I didn't like it and I didn't like it done to me. Why? Because it made the game more difficult, which is exactly what John Mahoney of Wales is doing to me here, dogging my footsteps and keeping between me and the goal. You have to be sharp to lose a man like that, disguising your intentions with little feints and darts, kidding that you're going one way before slipping away in another direction so you get half a yard of space on him. There were a lot more big scores in the old days before the advent of man-to-man marking, far more freedom of expression. But then Hungary thrashed England 6–3 and 7–1 in 1953 and 1954, and perceptions changed. A lot more thought went into English coaching expressly to avoid that sort of humiliation happening again.

Below Having a giggle with Roger Hunt as we walk off at the end of that tight clash with Spain. I have always had loads of respect for Roger. Some people think misguidedly that he was the one who replaced Jimmy Greaves in the England World Cup team, but actually he had earned his place on merit by scoring hundreds of goals for Liverpool over many seasons. Geoff Hurst was the man who came in for Jimmy and there was never any question that Roger would be left out. He was one of the most unselfish footballers I have ever known, being ready to run all day without getting the ball if it was going to help the team. His contribution to winning the World Cup in 1966 has been chronically underplayed. He's very modest, too, and has never been bothered by not being called a great player. However, I beg to differ. In my book, for both club and country, Roger Hunt was a true great.

Above I used to practise hitting through the top of the ball to keep my shots low, and this goal against Spain at Wembley in April 1968 was a perfect example. It was five minutes from the end of a European Nations Cup quarter-final first leg and the game was deadlocked at 0–0 when Bobby Moore tapped a free-kick into my path. I managed to swerve wide of some defenders and hit a right-footer across their 'keeper, Sadurni, and into the far bottom corner. I always tried to keep my shots down because I found it all too easy to blaze the ball into the stands. Even the ones which hit the roof of the net, and looked so spectacular, were meant to be lower.

Above It can't have been too often that Alf Ramsey was happy with third place, but there's a smile on his face as I leave the pitch after the 2–0 victory over Russia at the Olympic Stadium, Rome, in June 1968 in the European Nations Cup. People have called Alf cold, but he had his warmer side and he's demonstrating it here. He respected his players and always thanked them for their efforts, although he was never excessively effusive. But then, we wouldn't have wanted him to be. We knew exactly where we stood with him, we could rely on his complete fairness and integrity, and that was good enough for us. This game was a play-off between the losing semi-finalists after we had gone down by the only goal of a bruising battle with Yugoslavia. We should have beaten them but they had taken the view that they would win come hell or high water, by whatever methods they could get away with.

Opposite This is a passable illustration of my shooting technique. Notice that I have both feet off the ground, which is something which happens through your natural impetus if you follow through properly. Balance is all-important, though that is difficult to achieve when you are being tackled, so strength and fitness are needed to resist the physical challenge.

Above I don't know who was writing my script, but I was made up to score this goal on my 100th appearance for England, as captain for the night against Northern Ireland at Wembley in April 1970. Emlyn Hughes slung over a cross from the left, uncharacteristically Pat Jennings failed to take it cleanly and the ball ran loose for me to slide it into an empty net for the last goal in our 3–1 win. I remember the pitch was a mess – it wasn't the same after they'd allowed horses on it for the Horse of the Year Show – but I wasn't complaining. I knew I was a lucky man, lucky to have played with so many good players, lucky to have stayed fit, lucky that Alf kept picking me.

Right Strolling off the Wembley pitch after the Northern Ireland game and getting a pat on the back from a man who deserved a century of caps as much as anyone who has played the game. It's not because Gordon Banks is a good pal of mine that I describe him as the best goalkeeper I've ever seen, it's because that's the simple truth. He always made stopping a football look so easy. Lots of times when playing against Leicester or Stoke I smashed in what seemed like a perfect shot, only to be deflated as Gordon gathered it in as nonchalantly as if he was picking cherries. He never showboated, never threw himself around unnecessarily. He didn't have to because his positioning was so brilliant. When I was playing for England, we never despaired if an opponent got beyond our back line, because we knew there was always Gordon – and where there was Gordon there was hope.

Above I never minded playing a game for the press provided they didn't ask me to do anything *too* ridiculous. So when I reached my century of England caps and they wanted me to put

one on my head, then sit on the floor with the rest laid out to read '100', I agreed. After all, earning 100 caps was a big event at the time, with Billy Wright being the only England player to have reached the milestone before me, and I was really proud of the achievement. Whatever else, the pictures answered a couple of frequently asked questions. They showed that, yes, the players do receive real caps, and gave me the chance to explain that you got one for each tournament rather than for every match, so I didn't actually possess 100 pieces of headgear. Also they revealed how beautiful the caps are, made from velvet with silver braid by a company in Bradford. The picture was taken in a spare room at our former home in Lymm, Cheshire, but these days I keep them in my bank because they're so valuable.

Left I had a good friend, George Makey, who was one of the greatest workers for charity I have ever known. When I completed my century of caps, he had 100 commemorative plates made in Crown Staffordshire china and they were sold to raise money to buy children's electric wheelchairs, which were not available on the National Health. He also asked me to be chairman of Golf Fanatics International, which helped all sorts of marvellous causes, but it was George who did all the work. My part was just to turn up for the occasional round of golf on a Sunday. Sadly, George died a few years ago, but Norma and I treasure one of the plates, which we have at home and which reminds us of a wonderful man.

Above There was no club-versus-country conflict when Sir Alf Ramsey was England manager and Sir Matt Busby was in charge of Manchester United. The way the Old Man viewed it was that it enhanced the stature of his club for his players to become internationals and he was delighted to help Alf all he could. There was a deep mutual respect between the two men and I never heard of even a hint of discord. Alf worked very hard on his relationships with all the clubs and often when we stayed at Hendon Hall in north London I'd see him with a group of two or three First Division bosses. He had a certain way with him, and I'd say it was rare that he didn't get what he wanted. This occasion, though, was not directly to do with his England team, but a meeting in Fleet Street in November 1970 to discuss the setting up of a Football Hall of Fame.

Above Let it snow – it won't keep the England boys off the training pitch. One of the things which has always given our footballers the image abroad of being rugged and ultra-professional is our willingness to play in all conditions. And why not? It's a winter game, after all. Typically, if there was fun to be had then Jimmy Greaves was at the centre of it, and here he looks like he might be proposing a snowball fight to Norman Hunter. Meanwhile I'm wiping my nose ahead of the fray, while Gordon Banks is the lucky one, being equipped with a pair of gloves.

Above 'Back home, they'll be thinking about us . . .' Actually I could hardly blame the fans if this England World Cup song, recorded in a London studio before we went to Mexico in 1970, turned them off music for the summer. At the time it was the norm for an international squad to record a song before heading off for a tournament, and we were all in it together so there was no need for us to feel self-conscious. I don't think there were any of us who fancied themselves as singers, and it might have been just as well that we didn't really hear it being played, as we were in Mexico. Does it have pride of place in my record collection? Strangely enough, I think Frank Sinatra still has the edge! On a poignant note, it's so sad now to reflect that Emlyn Hughes (left), one of life's great enthusiasts, and trainer Les Cocker (second right) are no longer with us. The other lads in the choir are Ralph Coates (front left) and Peter Thompson (right).

Opposite Alan Ball was always a great man to have on your side, whether you were playing football or aces to kings. That's a game along the same lines as rummy, where a lot of the fun is in picking up new cards and making sure nobody else could see your hand. Sometimes we played in pairs and here Alan is 'pulling' for me as we wait for dental checks at Stanmore hospital ahead of the 1970 World Cup. Not that he was a really good card player; I never met a footballer who was. It was just something to pass the time while having a laugh. Alan was so bubbly, a little bundle of fun, and often he would tease me by holding a couple of cards back. Whatever he was doing, he was such an enthusiast and every day was like Christmas Day to him. I can hardly believe he has gone. He was always phoning his dad, Alan Ball senior, who managed various clubs. Alan loved football, his dad loved football, he loved his dad, and he talked about nothing else.

Two encounters with the Brazilian midfielder Clodoaldo in our closely contested group game at Guadalajara during the 1970 World Cup finals in Mexico, one rather more painful than the other. On the right, I'm getting off a left-foot shot from just inside the area, which obviously didn't go in because we lost 1–0, though it was an up-and-down match in which we had chances to win. Above, Clodoaldo has mistimed his tackle and sent me flying. The great myth about the Brazilian game is that they are all pure ball artists. In truth, they have always been as tough as any players on the planet, and their history is studded with magnificent defenders who were as ruthless as they come. For instance, during the 1958 World Cup in Sweden, Djalma Santos was the best defender on show, and he was not a man with whom it was advisable to take liberties. All the headlines went to Pelé and company, but the Brazilians understand that first you have to win the ball, and *then* you start to play.

Above I don't know how the hell I got into this position. Clearly there was a full-on collision with West Germany's Horst-Dieter Hottges in the World Cup quarter-final and we've both tumbled head over heels, but I don't recall the precise challenge during this quarter-final at Leon in 1970. I can be sure I wasn't injured, though. I was very fit and strong, and my balance was pretty good. If I did go over I knew how to roll with the impact, as did Hottges by the look of it.

Above right A study in concentration under pressure from German defenders in a game I had expected us to win.

Opposite When Sir Alf Ramsey pulled me off and sent on Colin Bell in the West Germany match, I didn't dream that I had kicked my last ball for England. I had been substituted fairly near the end in all the other games and it hadn't bothered me at all. I was nearly 33, there was the altitude to cope with, and as I didn't have any hair I could be troubled more easily than others by the heat. We were winning, and even though Franz Beckenbauer had just reduced the deficit to 2–1, I was confident that we'd be in the semi-final. I didn't argue with the manager – there was never any point! – although ironically I felt really fit and full of running. Of course, what happened next, with the Germans winning 3–2, was devastating. Then, on the way home, Alf asked me to sit with him and thanked me for everything I had done. He was sorry for the way the tournament had ended for us; it wasn't what he had planned. He didn't say he wasn't picking me again, but he didn't need to. He would be working towards the next World Cup, when I would be 37, so there was no way I could be there. That's how my England career came to a close, and I couldn't have a single complaint.

CHAPTER 9

Turbulent times

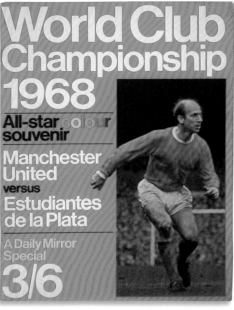

World Club
Championship
1968
All-star colour
souvenir

Manchester
United
versus
Estudiantes
de la Plata

A Daily Mirror
Special
3/6

Left I'd always thought I understood the difference between European and South American football, but when we played Estudiantes de la Plata in the World Club Championship in 1968, I found I'd been as innocent as a new-born babe. Matt Busby warned us that we were in for a hard physical contest, but that wasn't the half of it. In the first leg in Argentina they kicked blue murder out of us and Nobby Stiles was sent off in ridiculous circumstances. I wasn't used to being hacked when the ball was 50 yards away, and I carry the scar to this day. But they only beat us 1–0 so we were still within range.

Before the second leg they stayed in Lymm, near where I lived, and with the media describing them as animals, the locals expected to have monsters prowling their streets. In fact, our visitors mounted an unbelievable PR operation, smiling and engaging everybody, being nice to children, the whole works, and soon they were so popular that there were Argentinian flags on the village dustcart. Even Norma, my

wife, said: 'I thought these men were violent, but they're perfect gentlemen!' But then came the match and we were back in the war zone, being kicked from pillar to post. We lost 2–1 on aggregate, but we had learnt a lesson, albeit an extremely painful one.

Opposite top In the spring of 1969, we belied our indifferent League form to move within an ace of a second successive European Cup final. Having gone down 2–0 in Italy to AC Milan in the first leg of the semi, we overran them at Old Trafford but had nothing more to show for it than this goal scored after 70 minutes. I picked up the ball fairly centrally, took it to the right, then shot hard and high over 'keeper Fabio Cudicini, the father of Chelsea and Tottenham custodian Carlo, from quite a narrow angle. After that we attacked in waves but couldn't break through again, although Denis Law believes to this day that a shot of his crossed the line near the

end. When the final whistle blew I was cheesed off because I felt we'd performed far better than a 2–1 aggregate defeat suggests.

Above Nobby Stiles had been out all season and undergone two knee operations so he was delighted to be back, although the way he is hugging himself and the pained expression on his face does not suggest untrammelled delight on this perishing Turf Moor afternoon at the end of November 1969. These days the players would be wearing vests in the depths of winter, but it just wasn't done in our time. I can promise you we had nothing on under our shirts. I can't recall what Nobby was saying to me, which probably is just as well, but I'm certain that as soon as the whistle went he would have forgotten the temperature and thrown himself into the action. Sadly his knee was still not right – observe the bandage – and he managed only one more game before another lengthy lay-off.

Right When Wilf McGuinness took over from Sir Matt Busby as manager of Manchester United it was a strange situation for me. We had been pals ever since I'd arrived at Old Trafford and now he was my boss. He was giving the orders and I was taking them. It felt odd to me and it can't have been easy for Wilf, especially as things weren't going right on the field and the Old Man was still there in the background. Wilf's always been such an effervescent, enthusiastic character and you would never meet anyone who loved United more than him. Whoever replaced Sir Matt was always going to have problems, and sadly it didn't work out for Wilf. Inevitably he left but, happy to report, he has long since returned to Old Trafford to work in corporate hospitality, and our friendship has survived to this day.

Below When Wilf departed in December 1970 with United perilously low in the First Division, it was a difficult time for everybody at Old Trafford, but Sir Matt was waiting in the wings to resume temporary control. He still commanded the respect of all the players and in the short term he righted the ship. Relieved that United were climbing the table again are, right to left, myself, Denis Law, George Best, Sir Matt, Brian Kidd, Paddy Crerand and David Sadler.

Left and below I never enjoyed playing against Jack. If we were going to win I wasn't going to get a great deal of pleasure out of it because I knew that he would be left disappointed. I don't know if he felt the same but that was my take on it. When we went for a tackle, did it matter that we were brothers? Well, we would both expect the other to be professional and try to win the ball. If he did it unfairly, committed a foul on me, I would have been upset, but my brother was never a dirty player. Leeds had plenty of players with reputations for looking after themselves but when Jack gave away free-kicks I honestly believe it was through being clumsy rather than dirty. I might be mistaken, but in all the meetings we had on the field, I don't recall Jack fouling me once. Both these pictures were taken at Elland Road. Below, we're racing for a ball inside their penalty area in a game in January 1969 in which I scored but which Leeds won 2–1 on the way to their first league title under Don Revie. The photo on the left comes from another tight encounter during the following September which ended two-apiece, with George Best striking twice for United. Words, it would seem, were superfluous.

Right I thought I was in London for the opening of the Sportsman's Club one evening in November 1969 when I became the latest victim of Eamonn Andrews brandishing a distinctive red book for the television programme *This Is Your Life*. The other players were off to Blackpool for training and I was fed up because I was going to miss out on the trip to the Norbreck Hydro, one which I always enjoyed, instead having to head south along with Sir Matt Busby. As it turned out the lads weren't going to Blackpool at all, and they popped out to greet me after Eamonn had sprung his surprise. I was pretty dumbfounded at first, then a little embarrassed at being the sole centre of attention (as the photo on the right shows), but it was wonderful to see so many people who were close to me, including (in the photo below) my younger brothers Tom (left) and Gordon. Of course, Norma was there, too, and she had known about it all along without giving me the faintest clue. In the end I did enjoy it, though I have to admit I would rather have been playing football.

Opposite I loved it when United played at Loftus Road because nowhere else did the players come closer to the fans. It was such an intimate ground with hardly any distance between the touchline and the perimeter wall. To take a corner there was only a tiny run-up and I always held on to that wall to get my balance. If the referee hadn't blown for the kick to be taken then invariably the supporters would have a word. It was never nasty – most likely asking what I'd had for breakfast or some other bit of good-natured banter – and I enjoyed chatting back. As you can see here, sometimes even the ambulance men joined in. This one's probably having a laugh at a shot I had fluffed a few minutes earlier! And here's a sign of the changing times – look at the lad to my left, holding a rattle. These days he wouldn't be allowed to take it in. It would be classed as an offensive weapon.

Football-wise, the tightness of the Loftus Road pitch was a great advantage to Queens Park Rangers. It wasn't that it was intimidating, merely that the home team were used to it. It was possible for visitors to make something of it, though, as Peter Schmeichel once demonstrated with a brilliant piece of opportunism. When the Rangers full back overlapped, United's giant Danish 'keeper caught the cross which came in and before the defender had a chance to sprint back, Peter had thrown the ball well into the other half, putting the Londoners' goal under instant threat from the likes of Ryan Giggs and Andrei Kanchelskis. Now that's what I call a counter-attack.

Right At a troubled time in his life when some of his personal problems were beginning to spiral out of control, George Best could have done without a misunderstanding which led to his dismissal at Chelsea in August 1971. The fact was George had sworn at team-mate Willie Morgan and not the referee, but he could not convince the official and was ordered off. Clearly the Irishman was dazed by the decision and Tony Dunne (left) helped me to escort him away from the ensuing altercation. On this occasion, justice prevailed in the end, with the FA disciplinary committee accepting George's version and imposing only a suspended ban. But as far as the fans at Stamford Bridge that day were concerned, they had been deprived of watching one of the world's top footballers. Of course everyone, including the stars, has a duty to act responsibly, but sometimes when words are spoken in the heat of the moment, I think a little more perspective and cool judgement on the part of referees would help.

Opposite Even by the divine standards of George Best, it was one of the most coruscatingly brilliant pieces of work I had ever witnessed on a football field. It was October 1971, we were playing the unbeaten league leaders, Sheffield United, at Old Trafford and pretty late in the second half it was still goalless. We were second in the table and the crowd was getting a little bit frustrated as it looked like our opportunity to make up ground might be slipping away. That was the cue for George to pick the ball up on the halfway line, just to the left of the centre circle, and set off on a diagonal run to the right. He danced past one tackle, then slalomed beyond another defender, but by then he had been driven so wide under fierce challenge from a Sheffield man that a goal looked out of the question. But George could always surprise you, and suddenly he wrapped his foot round the ball to send a beautiful low cross-shot just inside the far post. It reminded me so much of the day he made me feel ridiculous in front of the Stretford End. Obviously George was a fantastic performer but he didn't always give you the ball. I said to myself that one day, when the game was safe and he looked for me to run into space so he could bounce the ball off me, I wouldn't do it for him. It happened against Nottingham Forest. He went all the way across the pitch and back again with the little full back Joe Wilson chasing him. I was blazing and made up my mind to stand still. As he came close to me with the ball on his right foot, I started to say: 'George, you greedy little . . . what a fantastic goal!' That summed him up for me, and it was much the same against Sheffield United. As I hugged him in breathless celebration in the late-afternoon autumn sunshine, with a bank of ecstatic fans behind us, I knew I had been close to something very, very special.

Above Those who prefer their referees to be unobtrusive would have been less than impressed by Roger Kirkpatrick. He was such a busy bee and he used to drive me potty. Mr Kirkpatrick was one of the most flamboyant officials I have ever encountered, full of extravagant gestures, running both forwards and backwards at high speed with his knees pumping like some cartoon character. The question I have to ask was this: did all this gesturing actually improve his performance as a referee? In this game at White Hart Lane in March 1972, I'm placing the ball for George Best, who wants to take a quick free-kick, while Mr Kirkpatrick – or should that be Mr Pickwick? – directs the traffic.

Above As captain of Manchester United, I was one of the first to welcome Frank O'Farrell to Old Trafford as the new manager in June 1971. Unlike his predecessor Wilf McGuinness, Frank was not one of the United 'family', but I nursed genuine hopes that he could set the club on the right track. But after taking us to the top of the table during his first autumn in charge, we fell away badly and he made an unhappy exit. Frank's approach to coaching was so different – some might call it modern – that I don't think a lot of people understood it. I got the feeling, too, that he never quite came to terms with the continued presence of Sir Matt, and it's certain that George Best's ongoing problems didn't make his life any easier. When Frank left I was sad that it hadn't worked out for him at Manchester United. He was a likeable, charming man and I never bore him any ill will.

Right Trainer Jack Crompton didn't think he was doing his job unless he brought us to our knees during our pre-season preparation at The Cliff. He was a fitness fanatic, the most demanding of taskmasters and tough as teak, which is not surprising given that he was the goalkeeper in Matt Busby's first great United team just after the war. In Jack's prime 'keepers were fair game for any opponent who fancied a physical battle, so they had to stand up for themselves or perish. He was unashamedly old-fashioned, a man of his time, so I don't know if all his methods were scientifically correct, but he was unswervingly loyal and I got on with him so well that later I took him with me when I joined Preston as manager. Here there's a smile on Jack's face, so his stopwatch must have told him I was doing OK.

Above A study in total absorption, with every shred of my being focused on what's going to happen next to that bouncing ball. It looks as though I might be about to head it, which explains the slightly apprehensive expression.

Opposite The Dell at Southampton was always a difficult place to pick up points, and United were involved in one or two gruelling physical battles in the compact little south-coast arena. From the expression on my face it would seem that this was one of those occasions, and that this particular challenge really hurt. Knees can go when you're tackled hard from that angle, but I was lucky enough never to suffer a serious injury so I must have ridden it. As an attacker I had to be able to survive this sort of thing and I was helped by having decent balance and carrying a little bit of stock on my frame. I always believed that the thinner lads, like Dennis Viollet and Denis Law, were far more prone to injuries because they didn't have the same protection. But taking the knocks is all part of the game and it wasn't a problem. Certainly it was never going to put me off football. This time as we went home rubbing our bruises, the pain was lessened by reflecting on our 5–2 victory, to which George Best had contributed a tremendous hat-trick.

Above Martin Buchan has the reputation of being a serious individual, but there's a smile on his face as he attempts – desperately, but no doubt in vain! – to intercept my high-velocity dash for the line during a light-hearted spot of tag rugby at the end of a training session. Martin was a thoroughbred footballer, Scottish and proud of it, and a strong, intelligent character who wasn't afraid to air his opinions, so I wasn't surprised when

he went on to become United captain for quite a few seasons. Unquestionably he was the pick of Frank O'Farrell's buys, but unfortunately for him he arrived during a tempestuous interlude at the club. He picked up a few medals, but a player with his ability deserved a lot more. These days Martin's working for the Professional Footballers' Association, based in Manchester, and he's doing a grand job.

Martin Buchan:

I'm not absolutely certain Bobby's got it quite right here. I know it looks like he might have outpaced me, but I think the angle might be deceptive, or maybe the light has induced a misleading impression. Mind, he is the only genuinely two-footed player I ever encountered, and the fact that he could go past an opponent on either side with equal ease made him exceedingly difficult to pin down, so I suppose it is conceivable he could have given me the slip! More seriously, I have great personal regard for Bobby Charlton, not only for his remarkable ability but for the fact that he pretty much took me under his wing and did his best to help me get used to life in Manchester when I arrived from Aberdeen in March 1972. He even took me to his home in Lymm and showed me around the village, but it was a long way from the training ground compared to what I'd been used to at Aberdeen, so I didn't settle there. Still, it was good of Bobby to take the trouble to make me feel welcome and I think that's the measure of the man.

sell-out 60,000 crowd would get decent value for money. It turned out to be as tough and competitive as any league or FA Cup encounter and I was booted up hill and down dale, even though it was my night. Celtic skipper Billy McNeill was very businesslike as we shook hands before kick-off, starting as he meant to continue, and the referee was Clive Thomas, perhaps the highest-profile official of his day. To be honest, I hadn't really wanted a testimonial because it seemed so final, but United explained that they couldn't allow others before mine was out of the way. So we went ahead and it was marvellous.

Opposite It was a thrill for me to find myself sitting in the dressing room at Goodison Park with two of Everton's all-time greats, Tommy Lawton (second left) and Joe Mercer. We were there, along with England captain Bobby Moore, for Tommy's testimonial match in the autumn of 1972, an event which I would not have missed for the world. My professional footballing uncles had always regaled me with tales of Tommy being the best header of a ball in the history of the game, and having watched some remarkable film footage of him in action, I'm not about to argue. Maybe he was born in the wrong era

Above I think my testimonial game was the only one I've ever known to finish goalless, but I couldn't have been more delighted with it. The last thing I wanted was a comedy match which ended up at 10–9, and that's why I invited Celtic to be United's opponents at Old Trafford in September 1972. You never get a friendly with Celtic and I was confident that the

because I believe he had to cope with some hard times, while if he was in his prime today he would be a global superstar and a multi-millionaire. The financial differential between then and now is so absurd, and although you can do nothing to change that reality, the least you can do is tell people how exceptional the likes of Lawton really were. Of course, Joe was an old chum of mine from his days of managing Manchester City, and we all had a tremendous natter. As for the fact I'm in a Liverpool shirt here, that wasn't a problem for me. There was no animosity between Manchester United and Liverpool in those days. None at all. I sported the shirts of Scotland, Celtic and many others in testimonials, and I was proud to wear every one of them.

Opposite The ground that Matt built. Tommy Docherty and Sir Matt Busby join me on the pitch at Old Trafford in the spring of 1973, shortly before my retirement. I know he was one of the most controversial characters in the game, but I never had a moment's problem with Tommy after he took over as United boss in December 1972. If I had a business appointment in London which might mean missing half a day's training, some managers might have stopped me, but he couldn't have been more accommodating, presumably trusting my judgement as an experienced professional. He took over a United team at the bottom of the table and steered us to safety, seeming not to be bothered by the presence of Sir Matt, who still spent a lot of time at the club.

Above If there's a football, and some willing kids, then why not have a game? I could never resist a kickabout and here I'm joined in a Fleet Street alleyway by none other than Sir Matt Busby and Derek Dougan, one of my colleagues, and a moving force, in the Professional Footballers' Association. I think I'm about to drop my shoulder and dart between the Old Man and the Doog, although the marking does look pretty tight . . .

Above Sir Matt Busby and I wet our whistles before a speaking engagement at the Anglo-American Sporting Club in Manchester. It's fair to say that neither of us were professional orators or natural comedians, but this dinner was for a good cause, and people were always ready to listen to the Old Man. He had that fantastically rich, mellifluous Scottish brogue which would entrance practically anyone within earshot. He just oozed authority, charisma and integrity, which served him so well in his dealings with footballers down the years. I've known players who have gone into his office with the intention of making a complaint, only to leave a few minutes later somehow feeling happy and grateful despite being rebuffed.

Right Blue skies over Old Trafford, a football under my arm and the new season just around the corner. What more could any man ask?

Above Before most of the last half-dozen matches ahead of my retirement as a Manchester United player in April 1973 I was showered with gifts. Often it fell to the opposing captain to make the presentation at kick-off, for example Jimmy Greenhoff when we visited Stoke City. Of course, a few years later Jimmy moved to Old Trafford and I recall thinking at the time that Tommy Docherty had made one of his shrewdest signings. There had been a period of a couple of years when Jimmy was probably the best striker in the country, and he was dreadfully unlucky not to be capped by England. His finishing could be explosive, but also he was blessed with a beautifully deft touch on the ball and such exquisite vision and awareness that he must have been a dream to play alongside. Though he was not in the first flush of youth when he arrived at United, the fans quickly adopted him as a hero and they adored him. He's a lovely modest character, too, and he remains a popular figure at Old Trafford as a match-day host.

Jimmy Greenhoff:

It was a proud moment for me to be asked to make that presentation to a man every footballer dreamed of emulating from the first moment he pulled on a shirt. Historically Stoke and United had close ties, with managers Matt Busby and Tony Waddington being close friends and the directors from the two clubs also being on good terms. So it didn't surprise me that they wanted to mark Bobby's imminent retirement.

Though I loved my time at Stoke, and was close to tears when I left, I had always had a very soft spot for United. Thus when Tommy Docherty took me to Old Trafford in 1976, I could hardly believe that I was soon to be changing in the same dressing room that Bobby Charlton had called home. What a role model Bobby was. Not only was he one of the most sensational players the world has ever seen, he was also a lovely down-to-earth bloke.

Opposite From the solemn faces of Sir Matt Busby and myself you might think we were about to face a firing squad, but actually it was much worse than that – I had just announced my retirement as a Manchester United footballer. Actually, I'm joking. It's true that I was about to leave, but really I wasn't down in the mouth about it. I was in my 36th year and I felt it was the right decision. I wasn't enjoying Saturday mornings any more. I wasn't excited by the prospect of the afternoon's match. I don't know why because I was still quite fit, but I moved very quickly from not even being able to imagine what it might be like not to play, to feeling that my lack of enjoyment was a definite sign that I should pack it in. I don't think it was because the club was going through a turbulent time, I believe it was just a matter of age. And in case you're wondering, I'm not sitting on Sir Matt's lap in this picture. It's just that the *Daily Mail* compacted the image for reasons of space and design. They say the camera never lies, but clearly there are times when it can be just a bit misleading.

Above Some 20 years after turning professional, I've still got my motor running in my last home game, against Sheffield United. The afternoon started with a generous ovation as I walked out on to the pitch, but ended in anti-climax as we lost 2–1 to the Yorkshiremen. I recall Tony Currie gave a terrific performance in midfield for the visitors and there were some observers who felt he might be a natural replacement for me at Old Trafford, but it never came to pass.

Left I felt it was usually referred to with affection, and I was never embarrassed by it, even on windy days, but in retrospect I can see why some people wondered why I persisted with the Bobby Charlton comb-over. I had always had a parting and I kept it for a long time, even when there wasn't much on top. But then one day I said to Norma: 'Can you cut this off for me, please?' It was the best thing I ever did. Still, not everyone has had a hairstyle named after them!

Above Maybe I'd put on a little bit of weight, perhaps I'd lost a yard of pace, but all the old instincts, to pass and to move, to dribble and to shoot, were intact. When I faced the final curtain at Chelsea on the afternoon of 28 April 1973 I wanted to end on a high note, I so much wanted to win, but we went down to a solitary goal by Peter Osgood. No matter. I'd had a fair old innings.

Opposite I'd always had a great deal of affection for Stamford Bridge and it felt an appropriate place to finish. I was given an unforgettable reception by the Chelsea fans, who had always been exceedingly kind to me. Now, after more than 750 games for Manchester United spread over rather more than a decade and a half, I was ready to embark on the rest of my life.

Above Bill Shankly holds the floor, as usual, after picking up the 1973 Manager of the Year award at the Café Royal, London. I had known Bill for a long time, and he had been a firm friend of my wife, Norma, ever since an unexpected visit to our home at Lymm, in Cheshire, early one Saturday morning. There had been a suspected prowler in the garden but on closer examination it turned out to be Shanks, who had been staying with his Liverpool team at a nearby hotel and was seeking a bit of enlightened football chat before leaving for his match. He certainly got that from Norma after being invited in for a brew. He was talking, talking, talking, and then suddenly Norma piped up with: 'How do you think the new substitutes rule is working out?' That was the moment he fell in love with her. A woman who talks football? Fantastic. After that, if ever Shanks saw Norma in a crowded room, he would make a beeline for her. He adored Matt Busby, too. Bill wasn't a boozer, the only time he took a drink being when it was poured for him by the Old Man. Also pictured at the Café Royal is Bob Stokoe (left), who was there to receive a special award for Sunderland's shock FA Cup final victory over Leeds that year. My brother Jack and I are both in attendance as rookie managers, he at Middlesbrough and I about to start at Preston.

Above There are two obvious questions here. Who is the mature-looking gent at the front of this group? And why is he sitting on the ground? It is my dear old friend, the football writer extraordinaire Geoffrey Green; and he is seated while others stand because he was, well, different. The occasion is the christening of his daughter, Ti, to whom I was proud to be the godfather – and thereby hangs a tale. We were on a night flight coming back from South America in the 1960s and neither of us could sleep, so we both repaired to the galley for a cup of tea. At least, I think it was tea. We ended up talking for hours and hours, and Geoffrey let me in on a secret. 'You're the first person I've told,' he confided, 'that I'm 60 years old and my wife is going to have a baby. I think we must have had a couple of drinks on the night in question!' In his next breath he asked me if I would be Ti's godfather and I was delighted to accept. I don't see her often these days, but it's always a pleasure when she drops by. Geoffrey died in 1990 and I do miss him. He was a fabulous writer, a true romantic who weaved magic with his words. Okay, he was a bit eccentric, but that was all part of his charm. That's his wife, Jenny, making sure I don't drop young Ti, and my wife, Norma, is behind Jenny.

CHAPTER 10

Deepdale detour

Above I was genuinely optimistic when I started work as manager of Preston in the summer of 1973, and if the grins were anything to go by, my players were in equally good heart. Preston has always been a traditional football town and I thought there was plenty to be achieved. But despite spending my whole life in the game, I found there was a deuce of a lot to learn. Instead of just looking after myself, suddenly I had to think for lots of different people, who all had their concerns and agendas. As Alan Shearer said when he took over at Newcastle in the spring of 2009, I had never been so tired in my life. Lining up in the back row, left to right, are: Jim McNab, John Brown, Alex Spark, Alan Kelly, David Wilson. Middle row: Alex Bruce, Neil Young, John McMahon, Stuart Baxter, John Bird, Eric Snookes. Front row: Alan Lamb, Graham Hawkins, Alan Spavin, Mel Holden.

Above I wasn't the only managerial hopeful going by the name of Charlton when the 1973/74 campaign got under way. Visiting me in my office at Deepdale is my brother Jack, who had recently taken over at Middlesbrough. As the season progressed we experienced vividly contrasting fortunes, with Jack's 'Boro romping away with the Second Division title and my Preston suffering the trauma of relegation. That *News of the World* football annual sitting on my desk looks well thumbed, but it would seem I didn't find too much inspiration within its pages.

Right 'If you think life at Old Trafford was tough, Nobby old pal, then you should try it at Deepdale.' I don't suppose they were the exact words I used to greet my old Manchester United team-mate Nobby Stiles when I signed him from Jack's team, Middlesbrough, just a few days into my first season at Preston's helm, but I'm sure he realised he was facing a challenge. I wanted his knowledge, his ability and his ceaseless enthusiasm, which I knew would offer us a priceless boost. He threw himself into it with a vengeance and, although his knee was troubling him sorely, he proved to be a fantastic influence. When it didn't work out for me at Deepdale and I left, Nobby stayed on, eventually going into coaching. I'm certain he could have played on longer if he hadn't done that.

Opposite Jock Stein said: 'Bobby, come and play for us,' and I didn't need any second invitation. It's not every day you get the chance to turn out for Celtic, and even though a season had passed since I'd laid aside my boots after leaving Manchester United, I felt fit enough to give a decent account of myself. In fact, I'd already announced I'd be making my comeback for Preston during the following campaign, and this underlined the rightness of that decision. The occasion was Ronnie Yeats' testimonial match in May 1974 and the venue was Anfield, where we – that's the other Celtic boys and me! – turned over Liverpool 4–1. I even managed to score the first goal in a contest which involved two proper teams, both playing seriously enough. OK, the Merseysiders had just beaten Newcastle to win the FA Cup and the holidays might have been on one or two minds, but they wanted to win, sure enough. It turned out

to be a wonderful night for Ronnie, who had been a magnificent servant to Liverpool and richly deserved this tribute.

Above I'd been managing Preston for nearly a season, and we were struggling. Then one of the coaches said to me: 'You're training with the players and you're as good as any of them, so why don't you play?' In a climate where there was not much money to spend, it made sense both for the club and me, so I decided to do it. I didn't ask for a playing salary, so nobody could call me over it, and I don't think it went too badly. I scored a handful of goals and did a job in central midfield, maybe helping some of my younger team-mates with my experience. Without being disrespectful to anyone, when you drop down a couple of divisions you have to make allowances for the different standard, and I had no problem with that.

Above The immediate aftermath of a glancing header. Maybe it was after seeing this photograph that I decided to get my hair cut.

Opposite I believe my expression offers eloquent testimony to my feelings on the day in August 1975 that I resigned as manager of Preston North End. I had quit on a matter of principle after discovering that the board were trying to sell my centre half, John Bird, to Newcastle behind my back. There was no way I could accept that and I told them straight away that I'd have to go. The players were shocked by my departure and wanted me to stay, even passing a vote of censure against the board. That was a lovely gesture on their part, but it was impossible for me to be manager and allow the directors to make team decisions. Any regrets? In retrospect, maybe I should have asked more people for advice, perhaps I ought to have gained some coaching qualifications, but having worked under some of the top men the game has known, I felt I knew what I was doing and just threw myself into it. In the end, despite everything, I did enjoy the experience.

CHAPTER 11

Glory days — and a knight to remember

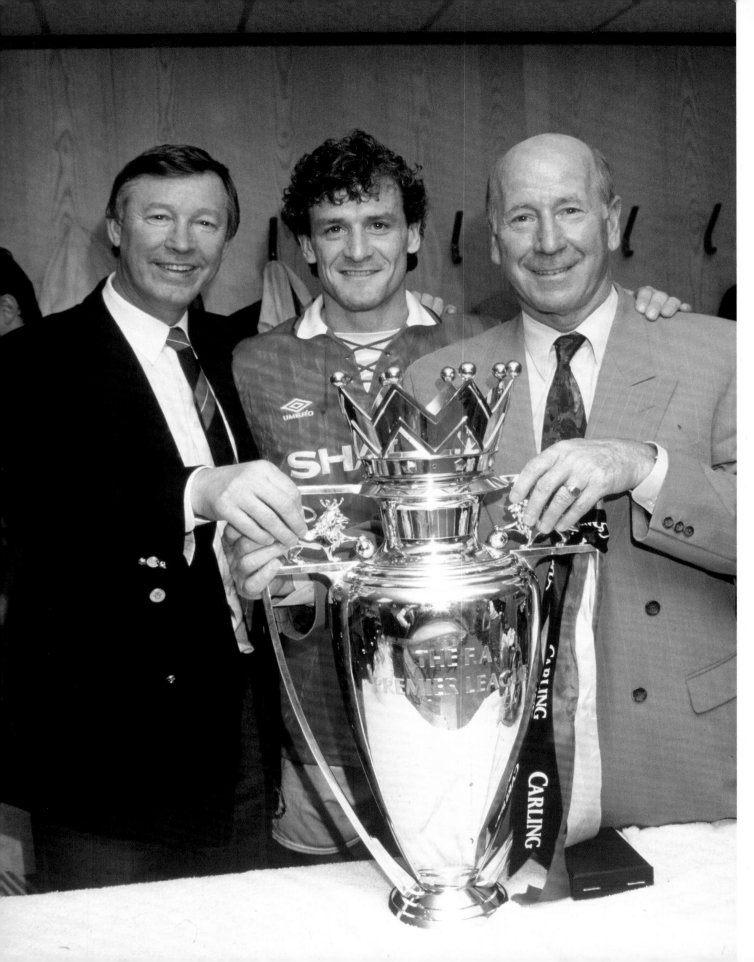

Opposite No matter how often you get your hands on a prime piece of football silverware, you never lose the hunger to do it again. Manchester United ended their 26-year league title drought in 1993, but when we retained the crown in 1994 there had been no loss of appetite among the likes of Alex Ferguson, our centre forward Mark Hughes or myself. Mark was a terrific performer, extremely tough and with bags of talent, who had played for United as a lad, then joined Barcelona. Alex was keen to bring him back and although usually it doesn't pay football folk to retrace their steps, this was the exception that proved the rule. Mark proved to be a magnificent re-signing, and only six days after this picture was taken he scored at Wembley as we completed the league and FA Cup double for the first time in our history. It was typical of Alex to get it right with Mark; our manager doesn't make many mistakes.

Above What wouldn't Alex Ferguson give for this feller to be a quarter of a century younger? Bryan Robson, a fellow North Easterner, was an inspirational figure at Manchester United. He was a top-quality footballer, but more than that he was a leader and a talisman. When United were up against it, so often he would win a tackle that should never have been won and you saw everybody in the team, and in the stands, be lifted by it.

Bryan wasn't bad, either, when he joined me on the leather sofa as my guest on the Sky television programme *Bobby Charlton's Football Scrapbook*. I did 50 or 60 programmes, each time talking about a particular match involving the visitor. Dickie Davies, the former ITV *World of Sport* presenter, acted as anchorman and saw that the chat never flagged. It was great fun and easy as pie. Who wouldn't want to natter at length about one of their best games?

Alex Ferguson:

What's it like to have such a figure around the club? I'm biased because since the day I've arrived Bobby Charlton's been my number-one fan. He's been great making my interests known in board meetings; if I said we needed to buy the moon Bobby would be the first with his hand up. The fact is that Bobby understands the game better than the rest. The others have a good idea of football, they're not short of that, they're all Manchester United men who have watched the team for a long time. But Bobby knows the game with every shred of his being. He's been a manager, and he knows the hard parts about dealing with players. He's been a great supporter of mine from the beginning and I'll never forget that. There was change needed to be made at our club when I came in and I needed Bobby beside me.

Above Some people have charisma. Often it's impossible to put your finger on just what it is that marks them out from the crowd, but they have that certain elusive something, and such a man was Eric Cantona. Just look at him here. Even when conducting a simple handshake, he holds himself so proudly. When we signed him we had to be prepared for the fact that he was a strong-minded lad, and we knew there might be awkward moments, but we felt we could cope with that. Eric arrived just as young lions like David Beckham, Nicky Butt, Paul Scholes and the Nevilles were bursting on to the scene, and he was the one who knitted them all together. He was as fast as anybody if he had to be, but ideally he liked to have these willing runners around him, so he could hold the ball and release it at just the right moment. He made everything happen and he played with a swagger reminiscent of Denis Law. Every time he scored a goal, his head went back, his chest went out and he stood there like a king, surveying all around as if it were his own private fiefdom. Eric Cantona was no ordinary footballer – and he was made for Manchester United.

Opposite Off with the fairies? Don't you believe it! This was taken just after Eric Cantona had scored the sensational goal which beat Liverpool right at the end of the 1996 FA Cup final, in the process securing our second league and cup double. It's fair to say I was pretty pleased with life, and why not? I'm a fan now, immersed in the action just as much as any other supporter. Eric's strike was just so wonderful, the way he adjusted his body in an instant to dispatch that perfect volley from the edge of the box. Things like that don't often happen in the closing minutes of a final so I reckon I was entitled to a little prance. Fantastic!

Above Aahh! Alfredo. When United entertained Real Madrid in the Champions League quarter-finals, Alfredo di Stefano (right) visited Old Trafford for the second leg and was greeted by two old United opponents from nearly half a century earlier, namely Bill Foulkes and myself. I have played against some tremendous footballers in my time, but I'd say Alfredo was the most intelligent and tactically aware, a play-maker who always told everyone else in his team what to do. I see him a lot at FIFA gatherings, and although he's now in his eighties, he's still as bright as a tack and knows what he wants. In fact, you might say as was his football, so is his character. He was particularly delighted to meet up with Bill again, referring to him as 'Foulk-ez.' Alfredo recalled that Bill was a very hard man, so there's absolutely nothing wrong with his memory!

Above Eight men for whom the word 'Munich' would forever hold nightmarish connotations, but who returned to Bavaria for a poignant reunion when the Champions League final was played in the city's Olympic Stadium in May 1997. All of us were survivors of the air crash which claimed 23 lives on that bleak afternoon in February 1958. We visited the modern hospital on the site of the one in which we were treated so expertly and with such compassion 39 years earlier. Left to right are Bill Foulkes, Harry Gregg, Dennis Viollet, Jackie Blanchflower, myself, Ray Wood, Kenny Morgans and Albert Scanlon. It offers a sobering reminder of the passing of time to reflect that three of this party – Dennis, Jackie and Ray – have died since making the trip.

Opposite Right Alex, this is how I see it . . . I'm not being serious, of course! Only when I'm asked do I offer my opinions to the best football manager ever. He doesn't so much consult me about things as tell me – and that's the way it should be. He's always absolutely in charge and makes all the major decisions. It's been one of the profound pleasures of my life to have spent nearly a quarter of a century in the same camp as Alex Ferguson. Back in the 1990s when, despite being a director, I still wore a tracksuit periodically on the United training ground, I might take some corners or try a few shots at Peter Schmeichel. But then I got to the stage where they asked me to send over some crosses and I couldn't reach the centre any more, so I stopped. There were times, too, when Alex might invite me to join a five-a-side. I must admit I still loved it, but then one day Brian McClair unintentionally hit me in the head with a shot that was so hard I went down. The imprint of the ball was on my face, much to everyone's amusement and, as I got to my feet, I said that perhaps the time was right for me to get out of the road here. Sometimes discretion has to be the better part of valour.

Left The lad who took this photograph after the barely believable climax of United's Champions League final against Bayern Munich in Barcelona in 1999 wrote in his caption that Alex Ferguson was waving to me. I can't verify that, although certainly I was there in the stand, clapping for all I was worth amid the bedlam that had broken out following Ole Gunnar Solskjaer's injury-time winner. But I do know it's a great study which captures the moment perfectly. Alex loves winning and he wears his heart on his sleeve. He just can't help it.

Alex Ferguson:

I bounce ideas off Bobby all the time. He tells me that if I want to throw my ideas at him, then he's ready to give his opinion. But he doesn't push himself. If you and I were standing at a reception talking to three or four people and Bobby walked in he's not the type to come across and burst into the company. You've got to drag him in because he's such a shy and humble person. People who can retain these qualities throughout their life are remarkable.

Right A trio of old workmates, back at the coalface. It was always a pleasure to be reunited with George Best and Denis Law, especially when the rendezvous was Old Trafford. This time we were receiving lifetime achievement awards during half-time in the match with Newcastle in August 2000. George was in fine form at the time, and just look at Denis, as jaunty and full of beans as ever. There was always a bit of a strut about him, and the fans loved him for it. Back in our days together as players, it was a perfect time. For about three years in the mid-1960s it felt like paradise. The fans flocked in, grounds were full wherever we went and United were on fire. People felt they had to go to every match in case they missed something extraordinary. Denis would grab a hat-trick, George would dribble past six defenders, and if I scored the odd goal I was pleased. You never knew what to expect with George. He could be so frustrating, but then the next minute he would turn a whole defence inside out. As for Denis, I knew fine well that if I went down either wing and got in a decent cross then he'd be on the end of it. As characters we were all different, but I think I'm quite close to Denis now, and I believe I'd have been close to George, too, if he were here. If only he was.

Opposite I don't think there's been another player in the modern era I've admired more than Paul Scholes, and one mild Sunday lunchtime at Old Trafford in October 2006, just a few moments before Manchester United were due to face their great rivals Liverpool, I was delighted to present him with a silver plate to mark his 500th appearance for our club. As always when this becomingly self-effacing young man finds himself in the limelight but away from the heat of the action, he was slightly diffident, maybe even a little bit nervous as he was confronted by the usual battery of photographers. He shot me a tentative glance as if to say 'Come on then, let's get this over so I can get on with my real job.' And when the game started, that's exactly what he did in his customary majestic yet matter-of-fact manner. As happens so often, Scholesy was the heartbeat of United that day as we won 2–0. He controlled the play from the centre of the park, scoring a goal just before the interval and finishing as undisputed man of the match. There is a purity about his understanding of the game, the way he always searches for the most incisive pass, the beautiful certainty of nearly everything he does. Watching Paul Scholes makes me feel young again, and for that I can only love him.

Paul Scholes:

Bobby Charlton's playing days at Old Trafford ended the year before I was born, but as a young United fan I was always aware of his fantastic achievements. That made it all the more astonishing when, once or twice, people have compared aspects of my game to Bobby's. Honestly, it staggers me that I have even been mentioned in the same breath.

As a director he's around the club a lot and when he comes in the dressing room he is a major influence. He never interferes, or gets deeply involved in football discussions, instead being content to remain in the background. There's no denying, though, that his presence is inspirational to us all. He's such a nice man, too, wishing everyone good luck, and certainly it produces a glow of satisfaction in me when he says 'well played' after a game. I love this picture of Sir Bobby making a presentation to me before my 500th game for United. I have it at home on my wall and it's something I will always treasure.

Above Perhaps it's not the first time in his life that Paddy Crerand has put his foot in it, but this is just plain ridiculous. Exactly why the four of us – Nobby Stiles, Paddy, Denis Law and myself – are convulsed with mirth is lost in the mists of time, but it might have something to do with the fact that our trousers are rolled up and we are dipping our feet into something messy. It seems that someone had the bright idea of establishing a walk of fame at Old Trafford, along the lines of the Hollywood version, and we were asked to get plastered to set the ball rolling. I've made a few enquiries and it seems that at some point the plan was quietly dropped. I think we can put that down as one of the merchandising department's least successful wheezes. But you can't win 'em all – and at least it gave us a laugh.

Paddy Crerand:

When I cast about in my mind for the finest footballers the world has known, players who stride across the pages of history and fulfil every requirement of greatness, in the way they handle themselves both on the pitch and off it, three names stand out. I think of Pelé, I think of Franz Beckenbauer . . . and I think of Bobby Charlton.

As a footballer for Manchester United and England he was sublime, and I consider myself lucky to have played alongside him for a lot of years. As a character he rejoices in universal respect, and rightly so. Not once have I seen his name in the newspaper for the wrong reason.

For all his public persona, I think he is quite a shy person, and some people take that as stand-offish. They could not be more wrong. When you get to know Bobby he can be extremely warm and funny, with a dry sense of humour. You should have seen him away from the pitch during our playing days, when he and Shay Brennan and Nobby Stiles were virtually inseparable pals. They did everything together.

Often it's my experience that the greatest players are the ones who say the least about themselves, and here Bobby fits the bill. That's his nature. Football is a working-class game, and he came out of a mining community, where respect was bred in him. That's part of Bobby and he'll never lose it.

Above Sometimes, when I have a quiet moment and there is nobody about, I like to wander on to the pitch at Old Trafford and just lose myself, gazing around me at the breathtaking edifice our ground has become. With my feet on the turf, which these days is lush and green even after a hard winter of football has been played on it, I lift my eyes to the stands towering above, and they inspire in me something which is not far short of awe. Up and up they go, so far towards the sky that it's easy to imagine they reach all the way to heaven. It's hard to picture how it looked to Matt Busby when he arrived at the end of the war, with the ground ravaged cruelly by Hitler's bombs. It even

seems surreal to me as I cast my mind back to how it looked when I saw it first more than 50 years ago, with the looming industrial chimneys, the bare terraces and the old-fashioned stands. It's the same place and yet not the same. Once when I was doing a foreword for a book with the distinguished writer Geoffrey Green, and he asked me what Old Trafford meant to me, I came up with the phrase 'Theatre of Dreams' because that's what it meant to me. Since then that description has been picked up and used all over, and I believe it is more apt than ever. It contains not only dreams, and hopes, but also precious memories. Truly it is a theatre . . . and it's alive.

Opposite Have you heard the one about the two Scotsmen and the Englishman? Both Alex Ferguson and Denis Law are full of banter and it's a joy to hear them when they get going. When Alex and I appear together, one of his favourite lines is: 'Do you know that Bobby and I have got 107 caps between us?' Now I know I've got 106 . . .

Above Ole Gunnar Solskjaer is a Manchester United hero of the ages for that unforgettable heart-stopping Champions League winner against Bayern Munich in Barcelona in 1999, but despite the fact that injury forced him to retire earlier than he would have liked, I'd wager that his overall contribution to the club has a long way to run. Because he's such a gem of a lad, liked by everyone who knows him, he's excellent as

an overseas ambassador, helping to make fans all over the world feel part of United, but also he's made a magnificent start to his day job of coaching the reserves. His team plays very bright football and he encourages his players to express themselves, which is exactly what Alex Ferguson wants. In his playing days, Ole was one of the finest snapper-up of chances I've seen. Sometimes at training I would stand behind the goal during shooting practice and throw back the balls which missed. When the Norwegian was in action I might as well have been back in the canteen having a cup of tea, because he was very rarely off-target. Here Ole and I are pictured launching the Manchester United *Opus*, a gigantic book costing several thousand pounds and intended for institutions rather than individual fans.

Above The faces say it all at the memorial service at Old Trafford in February 2008 to mark the 50th anniversary of the Munich air disaster. I am sitting between my wife, Norma, and Harry Gregg; beyond Harry is Albert Scanlon, a third survivor of the accident, and then, with head bowed, comes Alex Ferguson. I know Harry doesn't relish being called a hero, but it's difficult to find a more apt word, given the way he went back into the wreckage to pull people out. I don't know whether I could ever have done that. At the service, which I think the club handled admirably, Harry spoke movingly and with a tremendous dignity which has always been one of his most notable characteristics. It was an occasion that no one who was present will ever forget.

Alex Ferguson:

When Bobby came in to talk to the players at the time of the Munich anniversary, they were transfixed. You could hear a pin drop when he started talking. It was the first time anyone had heard Bobby really opening up about it. Some of the players knew a bit but not the details, or the emotions involved. You know fine well what football dressing rooms are like. If somebody comes in there's always a lot of nudging and messing about. Who the hell's this, that sort of thing. But there was none of that. They showed wonderful respect, every last one of them.

THE UNITED TRINITY
BEST   LAW   CHARLTON

Above With the backdrop of an azure Manchester sky, and with the sun glinting off the rich bronze finish, the statue entitled 'The United Trinity' outside Old Trafford, depicting George Best, Denis Law and myself, makes me catch my breath. It doesn't fall to many people to see a statue of themselves – usually such memorials are not put in place until the subject has passed away – and on the day it was unveiled, with my family beside me at the ceremony, I felt very proud and very humble. It wasn't an easy commission for the sculptor, Philip Jackson. Denis and I went to see him, and he took a lot of photographs, but at the beginning there was just a little something missing. For instance, my hair proved difficult, and so did Denis's, but eventually all the elements fell into place. These things can go wrong: so many statues are OK without quite managing to convey the correct essence, but I believe Philip, who is immensely talented, has got everything just right. I'm very happy that the statue is on Sir Matt Busby Way, looking across at an equally lifelike image of the Old Man, and I could not wish to be bracketed with two greater players. It is the ultimate honour.

Right It was throwing it down at Wigan on the Sunday afternoon in May 2008 when United retained the Premiership title and Ryan Giggs, who had scored a neat clincher in the 2–0 win, equalled my appearance record for the club. I'm wearing a coat while Ryan is soaked but he's hardly bothered about that on such a day. I can still recall the first time I laid eyes on him at a trial match at Littleton Road, just across from The Cliff. I was looking round for Alex Ferguson when I caught sight of this little lad running past people with the ball seemingly glued to his feet, then shooting past the goalkeeper. When I found Alex leaning on the goalpost at pitch 11, I said: 'Who's he?' Alex replied: 'That's Ryan Wilson [later he took his mother's name of Giggs]. We've just got him from City. I think he might do rather well . . .'

Right The rain was dripping down our necks, Alex's hair was plastered to his head and I don't suppose we looked particularly elegant in the raincoats we had been handed by the United kitman, Albert Morgan. But when the final whistle went at Wigan on the last day of the 2007/08 season and we had retained our championship, we weren't too bothered either by appearances or the elements. Alex Ferguson had done it again, and my mind flicked over his astonishing record since his arrival in 1986. I was always keen that we appoint him, and occasionally I have put in a word on his behalf in the boardroom, but I don't want to take any credit for what he's done. The truth is that our directors have so little to do because the manager is brilliant at his job. He has made our lives easy because we're winning. I can't thank him enough for what he's done for Manchester United.

Opposite Put it there, pal. Deep into the Moscow night, Cristiano Ronaldo and I are ready to celebrate after United have beaten Chelsea in the 2008 Champions League final. The lad's always polite, but he's a star and he knows it. He realises he's capable of doing things others can't do and he revels in it. Some of his former team-mates, say Ryan Giggs or Paul Scholes, are also superbly talented and they deal with it in a different way. That's not a criticism of Cristiano, just a reflection that people are not the same. His outrageous talent is blindingly obvious, but he's incredibly strong, too, and brave enough to take the cruel physical punishment that's often meted out to him. Hanging from my left hand is the medal handed to me when I led the team up to receive the trophy. I didn't want to take that walk because I didn't think the particular honour, immense though it was, should have fallen to me. That's why I didn't hang the medal round my neck, but kept it so it could go to the club museum where everyone could share it.

Alex Ferguson:

Bobby and I are football men, and we're football men of the old school. We don't have many differences, although he doesn't like me driving. He thinks my driving is the worst ever. Everybody says I'm a bad driver but I don't think so. When we're travelling, all we do is talk about the game. And we'll be talking about the young players. He loves them, you know. He loves to see young players coming through. He's been the course himself. I'm proud to say that Bobby Charlton is a good friend to me.

CHAPTER 12

The wider world

Above Some while after I had set up my soccer schools, this little lad from Essex came along and I picked him out as the winner of our end-of-course competition in two seasons out of three. Another coach said: 'Hmm, I don't know', but I could see he had both the ability and the desire. To make the prize really special I'd arranged to take the winning lad to Barcelona, where Terry Venables was manager. He was interested in this

boy, whose name was David Beckham, and later he tried to take him to Spurs. But both David and his dad were besotted by United and I mentioned the circumstance to Alex, describing him as a quiet lad who wanted nothing but to play football. Alex said: 'Get him in for a look.' And that's exactly what we did . . . and the rest is history, as they say. Manchester United and England aren't the only things David and I have in common. As you can see (opposite), we've both done a fair bit of modelling in our spare time. Here I'm wearing the 1966 World Cup-winning kit and have my boot on a shiny leather ball from that era, while David projects the modern look. I suppose I should point out, before someone else does, that the contrast extends to the waistlines, too.

Below It's true that I recognised a huge talent in David, but I couldn't possibly have envisaged that the young Beckham would grow up to win a century of caps for England. I have got to know him very well down the years and I was delighted when he asked that I should make the presentation when he reached the milestone on the night England faced the USA at Wembley in May 2008. When I handed him the case containing the special gold-coloured cap, he thanked me in his usual quiet way. A lot has happened in his life, but essentially he's an extremely decent person, a real family man.

Above I'd been fortunate enough to be on the receiving end of quite a few trophy presentations at Wembley in my time, but never before had I been the person handing over the prize. It was a huge honour to be asked to deposit the Charity Shield into the care of Nottingham Forest skipper John McGovern in 1978. England goalkeeper Peter Shilton is next in line and FA secretary Ted Croker is on my left, sorting out the medals.

Opposite We were both long retired, but it was tremendous fun for Jack and I to put on 1966-type England shirts and turn out for our country against West Germany once more. It was pretty satisfying to finish on the winning side again, too, this time by a 6–4 margin, even if the result was of no consequence. The game took place at Elland Road in the summer of 1985 to raise money for the victims of the Bradford fire, and this shot was taken before the game. Afterwards, I guess, we'd have been too knackered to stand up in front of the camera.

Above I've been lucky in life and been accorded many honours, but I don't think any of them have been quite as unexpected as a place in the National Portrait Gallery. In all honesty, though, I must point out that the picture was commissioned by British Gas, with whom I was working on my soccer schools at the time, not merely to have me immortalised in oils but as a commemoration of our whole World Cup triumph in 1966. When it was unveiled a few of my England team-mates turned up to support me and, not surprisingly, there were one or two irreverent remarks, notably from George Cohen (left), who asked why there was a halo around my head. I explained that it was no such thing, merely the artist's way of showing movement. Maybe the moon behind me is symbolising a football, which I have just nodded towards the top corner. The other art buffs who stopped by were Ray Wilson (second left) and Bobby Moore.

Above More than half a lifetime on from beating West Germany on that sunny Wembley afternoon that still glows so brightly in our memories, the World Cup winners remain a tight-knit bunch. So when something happens to one of us, as it has to Bobby Moore and Alan Ball, it really hurts us all. We don't live in each other's pockets but we do see each other a lot, taking it in turns to organise regular reunions, each in our own part of the country. It's not just for the winning team but for all the lads in the squad, and we were delighted when George Eastham came over from South Africa to attend in 2008. Actually this gathering in 2002 *was* only for the team and was part of a national campaign to lower cholesterol. They did tests on all of us to see if we needed to lose weight, and I was relieved to discover that I didn't. At the time, we had already lost our skipper, but little Alan Ball was still with us. Standing, left to right, are Nobby Stiles, Roger Hunt, Gordon Banks, my brother Jack, George Cohen and Ray Wilson. Sitting are Martin Peters, Geoff Hurst, Alan and myself.

Above A typically exuberant greeting from Pelé at the opening of the 2006 World Cup. I see him a lot because we're on the same FIFA committee and he's always the same. Always smiling, always immaculately dressed, and always late! He projects himself – that's the nature of his personality – and he's good fun. He's the one who came up with the description of football as 'The Beautiful Game', and it's certain that nobody played it more beautifully than Pelé. Often I am asked who was the greatest player of my lifetime, and I have to say Alfredo di Stefano was the most intelligent, and maybe Diego Maradona was the fastest with the ball under complete control. But when you come to the one with the most breathtaking natural gifts, there can be only one answer – and it is Pelé.

Above I don't know who's cracked the joke here, Princess Anne or George Cohen, but it seems to have gone down pretty well. The Princess is tremendous fun and she understands sport and sportspeople, having tasted plenty of success herself in international equestrian events. We're enjoying ourselves here at the sports writers' golden jubilee ball, where the standard of badinage was as rarefied as you might expect.

George Cohen:

This made me chuckle. Bobby had asked if the Queen Mother enjoyed a gin and tonic, and Princess Anne replied that her favourite was something else. I can't remember what it was exactly, but it seemed such an outlandish mixture that everybody laughed. Princess Anne was so approachable, no stick-in-the-mud, very much at ease with a roomful of footballers. As for Bobby, he was always essentially a quiet fellow, not one to put his opinions forcibly but, like the rest of the 1966 England team, he was a terrific professional who did what Alf Ramsey told him. As an opponent he was a handful, especially when he played in central midfield. He didn't favour one foot or the other, which meant that he could go past people on either side, and he was like lightning over the first 15 yards, so once he was past you wouldn't catch him. During his spell as an outside left he faced me directly, and in that wide position next to the touchline I could try to usher him into negative situations. But like all great players, you might hold him for 99 per cent of the game, but in that final one per cent he'd crucify you.

Opposite If I'm absolutely honest, golf used to mean a lot more to me than it does now. I don't play anything like as much as I did because I don't have the time. Back in my footballing days, I didn't play as much as some of the lads because I felt it took something out of me. In 1963 when we beat Southampton 1–0 in an FA Cup semi-final at Villa Park, I was on the left wing facing Stuart Williams, a fine full back but one who was approaching the veteran stage. With all due respect to Stuart, I would have expected to have been able to outpace him, but I was unbelievably sluggish and wondered what was the matter. After mulling it over – and maybe I was just making an excuse – I blamed it on my round of golf a couple of days earlier. Football's a quick, instinctive game, while golf is methodical, slow, contemplative, and I believe both mind and body can be affected. Matt Busby wasn't against it but, since football has been approached more scientifically, golf has fallen out of favour. Certainly Alex Ferguson won't let his lads play. A lot of people who love golf laugh at this theory, but I can see some

sense in it. Of course, I don't have to worry about any of that now and I do enjoy the occasional game. Here I'm aiming to lift my second shot on to the 17th green during the Alfred Dunhill Links Championship at Kingsbarns, Scotland, in 2006.

Above There are plenty of magnificent causes in the world, but one which really strikes a chord with me is the Laureus Sport For Good Foundation, which does a huge amount globally to help under-privileged children. Founded by the South African businessman and philanthropist Johann Rupert, it doesn't just hand out cash. There has to be a good idea in existence, then Laureus helps it to develop before eventually handing it over to the community involved. Rupert has attracted as active supporters many top names from right across the spectrum of international sport, as can be seen from this line-up at the Laureus Golf Challenge in Monte Carlo in 2003. Left to right are Boris Becker, Franz Klammer, Ian Botham, Dawn Fraser, Gary Player, Johann Rupert, myself and Kapil Dev.

Above 'Here are two familiar faces!' Those were the words used by Nelson Mandela to greet Alex Ferguson and myself when we met him in Johannesburg during United's pre-season tour of South Africa in 2006. I could hardly believe my ears. To think that such a truly great man, an inspiration to everyone, who had been subjected to many years of some of the worst suffering imaginable, and yet never had a bad word for his persecutors and retained his incredible dignity, should recognise a couple of football people from Manchester pretty well beggared belief. He was a bit frail on his feet but his voice was very strong as he thanked me for the plaque I presented to him, and he seemed to know a bit about United. Meeting such a man made us feel humble, and placed mere sporting concerns in their proper perspective.

Opposite I might look a trifle daft in this kit, but I couldn't care less because I was publicising a cause which is very dear to my heart. The picture was taken at the House of Commons following a meeting aimed at helping to eradicate the evil menace of landmines all over the world. Nobody argues about the essential rightness of this crusade, but the sorry truth is that countries will never stop laying them because often mines are used purely defensively. Despite that, it's got to be wrong for governments to sit back and say it's inevitable that when a particular war has moved on then children are going to walk under trees and have their legs blown off. I have visited Bosnia and Cambodia to find out more, and was horrified to discover that it can take two or three days to disarm a single landmine. Given the vast number of mines in existence, at the present rate of progress it would take more than 100 years to clear those in Cambodia alone. So while accepting that we'll never stop the use of mines, we must work towards getting rid of them more quickly. Some fine minds are striving towards that end and we must work and pray for a breakthrough.

I love working with kids, it is a lot of fun. Maybe it's because I'm like a big kid myself, but I've never had trouble communicating with them. I've always wondered why people find it difficult. All you do is make sure you don't patronise them, but talk to them as if they were adults, then you know fine well that they are listening to you. Kids are like sponges, they soak up new information and they're so quick. If I ever say the wrong thing around my grandchildren then they're on it in a flash. When I started my soccer schools I would start off with a little speech at assembly and I found out that football is a universal language. People can communicate through football who can't communicate in other ways. You just put a ball down and you're away. If you don't believe me, just send along a politician and send along a sportsman, and see which one makes the best progress. And as I hope is clear from these pictures, I enjoy myself as much as the kids. **Above** Going for a header at a major Laureus project in Montevideo, Uruguay. **Left** A soccer school session at Holyrood in Edinburgh. **Opposite** Showing genuine amazement at the ball skills of a youngster at an orphanage in Guangzhou, China.

I'm not someone who relishes chat-show interviews, but the first volume of my autobiography, *My Manchester United Years*, was out in the autumn of 2007 and, not unnaturally, the publishers wanted me to publicise it. I wouldn't have refused Michael Parkinson anyway because he's a good friend from a long time ago and is always welcome at Old Trafford. He knows the game of football and he knows his own game, too, putting people at their ease and gauging whether to let you expand a story or to butt in. I thought it all went off very well, thanks hugely to Michael, who just let me tell my own story. But I won't be looking for a job on the box. I'm not quite as photogenic as Joanna Lumley, one of my fellow guests. I had met her once before and knew she was a lovely person who cares a great deal about a variety of causes. She should be proud of her campaigning work in 2009 to ensure justice and settlement rights for veteran Gurkhas.

Sir Michael Parkinson:

When I got to know Bobby in the 1960s, he was always a bit shy and he was married, so he was never part of the social whirl in Manchester. But when he came on the show he was very easy to work with, maybe a tad nervous at first, but he has become more assured down the years. He proved an interesting and reflective interviewee, well worth listening to, and he mixed comfortably with the other guests, Richard Attenborough and Joanna Lumley. Bobby has become a national treasure who is held in colossal respect wherever he goes, and I think it's fair to say there was immense mutual admiration. I have always been fond of him as a character, and as a footballer, unquestionably, he remains one of the greatest we have had. Bobby Charlton would walk into any England team of any era.

Opposite I got the old legs working again for probably the best pub team in the world. This was a television advertisement for Carlsberg which had Bobby Robson managing a side against a real-life Sunday morning team in London. I was lining up alongside the likes of my brother Jack, Alan Ball, Bryan Robson and a starry collection of other internationals. The banter in the dressing room was brilliant and we all had fantastic fun, but I don't think I'll be signing a long-term contract . . .

Above What was the last goal I ever scored that was captured on camera? It's got to be the one in the TV advert for Actimel, the health yoghurt. For those who haven't seen it, the sequence was shot in a little park in Moss Side, Manchester. I'm strolling along with my whippet, just pausing to look at some kids playing football, when the ball lands at my feet. One of the lads, a smashing little actor called Jordan Hill from Bury, hollers out: 'Hey, Grandad, give us our ball back, please.' After that, the director's instructions were these: 'I want you to knock it from your left foot to your right, and then from 30 yards I want you to hit it into the top corner of the net.' I told him he might have to wait a bit! I had my ordinary shoes on, it was wet and they put a puddle in my way to make it more difficult. I thought I was going to be there all day, but after about ten efforts I whacked one just right and it flew into that top corner. The 'keeper didn't smell it. Straight away the director yelled, 'Cut!' And that was it. A few people have doubted that it was really my shot, but I can assure them it was. I even wondered about entering it for goal of the season . . .

Above Hamming it up in pantomime style with a couple of lads who seem as though they might be able to look after themselves. I don't think my puny left hook would do me a lot of good if Frank Bruno or Henry Cooper were really after my blood, but there's not much chance of that. Frank's a nice man and Henry's one of my best pals. In our time we've done a bit of work for the Royal Variety Club and it's always a pleasure to catch up with him. The thing about Henry, he's such a genuine character. All down the years, he hasn't changed a scrap, always open, friendly and ready for a laugh.

Opposite Paul Gascoigne's got into a few scrapes in his time, but I'm not sure that everyone is aware that he's always been such a willing worker for charity. Here he's accepting his medal from me after playing for England against the Rest of the World as part of UNICEF's Soccer Aid campaign at Old Trafford in May 2006. He loves the comradeship of being around footballers and essentially he's a lovely lad. I know he has to fight his personal demons and I hope he can overcome them. The game will always remember him, that's for sure.

Opposite It shouldn't happen to a dog. Obviously I'd be guilty of the most immense hypocrisy imaginable if I didn't admit that I felt like raising the roof when John Terry hit the outside of Edwin van der Sar's left post from the penalty spot in that tumultuous shoot-out at the Champions League final in Moscow in May 2008. The Chelsea skipper's slip kept United's hopes alive, then Ryan Giggs and Edwin did what was necessary to lift the trophy. But for all the joy that engulfed me when the glorious deed was done, I couldn't help but feel a searing shaft of sympathy for poor Terry, an honest professional and a valiant servant to his club who didn't deserve to suffer in such a demoralising fashion. That's why, when I met him before he captained England against the USA at Wembley a week later, I took the opportunity of offering a word of consolation, adding that I believed his day in the European sunshine would come. He said he had put his devastating miss behind him, but clearly he was still smarting from the experience. Every footballer who has ever taken part in such a nerve-shredding showdown could only feel: 'There but for the grace of God.'

Above This fur hat is one of the best things I ever bought. I picked it up at Kiev airport on the way home from a Champions League game with Dynamo nearly ten years ago. The directors tend to leave ahead of the team to get to the airport and while we were waiting for the players to arrive, I noticed that the shop was open, even though it was the middle of the night. I had been so cold at the game that when I spotted this hat I snapped it up, and it's fantastic. It pulls right down over my ears. One day at Villa it was absolutely perishing with an east wind swirling into the stand and people were coming up to me and saying: 'Can I buy your hat?' No chance! It only cost a tenner and I should have bought a dozen. I'd have made a fortune.

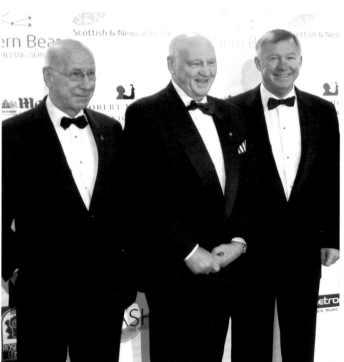

Left Bobby Robson was a wonderful person, one of the most courageous I ever met. He fought cancer for more than 15 years, but he kept fighting and never seemed to think about himself. What motivated Bobby was his drive to raise as much money as he could for other sufferers, and Alex Ferguson and I were delighted to be able to help out at this event in Durham. Bobby and I came from the same part of the world and we went back a long, long way. He was a great lad, always so positive and absolutely football-mad. People will remember him forever.

Above left Taking a moment for reflection in Manchester Town Hall before the morning press session ahead of my investiture with the Freedom of the City in the spring of 2009. I've been lucky and have not been short of awards and presentations, but I can't think of any I've felt better about than this. Manchester has been my workplace pretty well all my life and the people there have been fantastically good to me. When I arrived as a shy 15-year-old in 1953, and was met at the train station by Jimmy Murphy, I could never even have dreamed that one day I might receive such an honour. Manchester has always been a

vibrant place, a down-to-earth working community, and while it used to be black with pollution, a wonderful job has been done in cleaning it up. One thing that stands out for me about my adoptive city is that it's never afraid to try new things. It's said that Manchester builds everything and London markets it, and there's no question about where I prefer to be. I realise the significance of this award and I was humbled to receive it. Mind, it is purely symbolic, so there'll be no question of driving my livestock down Deansgate.

Above It was a family affair, and that was exactly how I wanted it. I am flanked by my three grandchildren, William (left), Robert and Emma. Behind us are my elder daughter Suzanne, the Lady Mayoress Mrs Irene Etchells, my younger daughter Andrea's husband Andrew Balderston, the Lord Mayor of Manchester Councillor Mavis Smitheman, my wife Lady Norma and Andrea.

Above right Sampling the awesome atmosphere of the Theatre of Dreams with my friend James Lawton, who did such a fantastic job on the two volumes of my autobiography.

The skilful way that he structured the story, and the flair and understanding which infused his writing, especially in some of the most emotional passages, moved so many people to tears, and it's down to him that *My Manchester United Years* won an award as the best sports autobiography of the year. For my money, Jim's the top football writer of the lot and he's always welcome at Old Trafford.

James Lawton:

Assisting Bobby Charlton in the telling of his life story, over two volumes, was a great challenge, one exceeded only by the sense of privilege and responsibility that accompanied it. I wanted, desperately, for the work to reflect both a wonderful career, arguably the most heart-warming in the history of English football, and the unassuming modesty that accompanied every majestic stride of it.

It was a great relief when critical reaction suggested this ambition had been achieved. Best of all, though, was the great man's generous conclusion that, after all the hours we had spent together, he felt his story had been truly told.

Jack Charlton:

Bobby was one of the best players in the world for a lot of years. I'd put him with the greatest there's ever been. It has always amazed me when people have put Pelé, or Eusebio, or di Stefano, up a little bit above Bobby. He was just tremendous. I was very pleased and very proud to have a brother like him.

Opposite There is no one on earth I would rather have received my lifetime achievement award from during the BBC *Sports Personality of the Year* show than my brother Jack. He and I are still close, no matter what exaggerated things people have written about our supposed differences. I think I'm getting pretty good at controlling the tears these days, but I have to admit they weren't far away when Jack was speaking with such emotion about the days when we were growing up together. It was a marvellous evening and the ovation I received was unbelievable: it just went on and on. I was a bit embarrassed and under my breath I said to the compere, Gary Lineker: 'Can we stop it now?'

Left When it was my turn to speak, I was anxious to say something about Liverpool, where the show took place. Sometimes people can get the wrong impression of the place when the bad things, which actually plague every city, are highlighted and dwelt upon. Liverpool is a lovely, warm and vibrant city, similar to Manchester in many ways despite all the fierce competition. Sometimes the rivalry between a minority of the United and Liverpool fans has gone too far, and I think it's time for all people from both ends of the East Lancs Road to move beyond that.

CHAPTER 13

Nearest and dearest

On the verge of matrimony in the summer of 1961, we were as overjoyed and excited as any young couple could be. Norma was wonderful at sorting out all the little details that are so important to the great day running smoothly – like checking our wonderful wedding cake had the correct number of tiers and making sure that I'd read all the cards.

Opposite The date is 21 July 1961; the place is Middleton in north Manchester; the occasion is the happiest day of my life. As we make our way to the car after our wedding ceremony, Norma looks absolutely stunning. She always has. She still does. There was quite a crowd of well-wishers in the street and the churchyard, and people were peering out of upstairs windows to catch a glimpse of us. I didn't mind seeing so many folk there. I understood that footballers lived their lives in the limelight, especially if they happened to play for Manchester United. But I must admit I felt a bit guilty that some of the youngsters were hanging on to the gravestones as they crowded round to watch us come out of the church. Of course, they didn't mean any disrespect, but I didn't want anyone to be upset. After the big day we just had time to squeeze in a honeymoon in the South of France before it was back to Manchester for pre-season training.

Left My daughters Suzanne (left), who was six, and four-year-old Andrea with Norma and me outside Buckingham Palace on the day I received my OBE in 1969. After the ceremony we took them to lunch at the Dorchester, and on the way home we asked them what was the best part of the day. Andrea had no doubts: 'It was that nice café we went to!' I know I'm biased but I do think the girls looked a picture, and so many people told us how smart they were, how unusual it was for girls to be dressed like girls in proper frocks and with pretty hats. Mind, I can't claim any of the credit for that. As ever, Norma had done a fantastic job.

Left We were in the kitchen having our breakfast when the registered letter arrived to inform me that I'd been chosen for a knighthood. The first thing we did was ring our daughters – Andrea greeted the news with a full-blooded scream which almost blasted the phone out of my hand. Later Norma and I went outside and had our pictures taken by the newspapers and this is one of our favourite shots.

Opposite The big day at Buckingham Palace. You can't buy a knighthood and, generally speaking, it's something the public wants to give you, so how could it be anything else but marvellous? I have never needed or had any aim to become an OBE, a CBE or a knight, but I appreciate these honours for what they are and I have always maintained they are as much for the game as for me. I just do my best to make sure my pals still call me Bobby, although some insist on the Sir. Of course, my wife became Lady Norma – that was the best part. When she married me I don't suppose she ever dreamed she would end up with a title, but it was well within her range!

Right Holding your first grandchild is a very special feeling and I can thoroughly recommend it. Welcome to the world Robert Harry Brown, the son of my lovely girl Suzanne.

Below The best hat-trick of my life, my three grandchildren. That's Emma and her brother William – Andrea's pair – on the wings, and Suzanne's Robert in the middle with me. I just hope they appreciate what they've got their hands on in the Old Trafford boardroom. They're all smashing, and I know the boys won't be jealous if I tell a little story about Emma. One day when she was only three I asked her if she wanted to come out into the garden to chase after a ball and she said: 'OK Bobby.' I said: 'Bobby? What do you mean, "Bobby"? I

thought you called me Grandad.' But then she gave me this outrageous wink as she added: 'Charlton!' Certainly we had never regaled her with tales of my football career, but it seems she'd heard about it at nursery school and bided her time before letting me know she knew. At this point, if anybody had the slightest doubt, I own up to being a doting grandfather.

CHAPTER 14

And finally...

The years are flashing past with alarming speed, but it has been the most wondrous of adventures. There have been dark, bleak times for sure, but also many moments of pure light and joy. I'd like to thank everyone who has shared it all with me and made my life in football – and beyond – such an overwhelmingly rich and fulfilling experience.

I am more than happy with my lot in life. I think these pictures demonstrate that better than any further words I can say.

Acknowledgements

For their love and inspiration, as always, my wife, Lady Norma, and my family.

For his gracious foreword, Ryan Giggs.

For scratching their heads and coming up with such generous reflections, Sir Alex Ferguson, Paul Scholes, my brother Jack, Denis Law, Nobby Stiles, Bill Foulkes, Roger Hunt, George Cohen, Johnny Giles, Paddy Crerand, David Sadler, Wilf McGuinness, Jimmy Greenhoff, Martin Buchan, Bryan Robson, Sir Michael Parkinson and James Lawton.

For the splendid photographs, Andy Cowie and all at Colorsport, Alan Pinnock and Greg Hill of the *Daily Mail*, David Scripps and Vito Inglese of the *Daily Mirror*, Hayley Newman at Getty Images, Lucie Stones at the Press Association, John Jeffay at the *Manchester Evening News*, George Herringshaw at Associated Sports Photography, and Neil Gee.

For ensuring everything went smoothly during the production of this book, David Wilson, Rhea Halford and Jo Whitford at Headline; for designing its layout so attractively, Dan Newman; and for casting his experienced eye over the manuscript, Jack Rollin.

For looking after my collaborator, Ivan Ponting, I'd like to thank Pat, Rosie and Joe Ponting, Cliff Butler of Manchester United, Les and Teresa Gold, and David Welch.

For providing Ivan and myself with the ideal place to do our work, everyone at Mere Golf and Country Club.

Picture credits

Action Images 258

ASP 124, 172 (bottom)

Courtesy of Cliff Butler 81 (top right and bottom right)

Camera Press 232–3, 246–7, 252

Courtesy of Sir Bobby Charlton 21, 28 (left), 211, 264–5

Colorsport 14–15, 16, 18–19, 48, 50 (bottom), 67, 75, 80, 82, 90 (bottom), 95, 100 (bottom), 101, 105, 123, 195, 204 (bottom), 207, 208, 217, 238–9

Corbis 50 (top), 262

Daily Mail 39 (top), 45 (bottom), 49 (top), 53, 56–7, 63 (top right), 71, 85, 92, 127, 135,139 (left), 168, 174, 177 (bottom), 192 (bottom), 199, 200 (top), 202, 204, 206, 215 (top), 216, 219, 228, 242 (top), 253, 258, 270–1

Courtesy of Neil Gee 265

Getty Images 3, 8–9, 20, 31 (top), 32, 38, 58–9, 63 (top left), 66, 68, 70, 78 (bottom), 83, 86, 87, 90 (top), 106, 110, 117, 120, 125, 126, 132 (top and bottom), 137 (bottom), 138, 146–7, 148–9, 154–5, 156 (bottom), 164, 173, 176 (bottom), 190 (top), 196, 201, 210, 222, 227, 231, 235, 236–7, 242 (bottom),243, 244, 248, 250–1, 254 (top), 255

Manchester Evening News 33, 34, 49 (bottom), 52, 157, 163 (bottom), 190 (bottom), 225, 226, 234, 259, 263, 264 (top), 267, 274 (top)

Courtesy of Wilf McGuinness 12, 17, 36–7, 163 (top)

Mirrorpix 10–11, 13, 24–5, 26–7, 28 (right), 31 (bottom), 35, 40, 42, 52, 56, 60–1, 62, 63 (bottom), 64, 72 (top), 73, 74, 84–5, 93, 94 (top), 96–7, 100 (top), 102–3, 104, 108–9, 111, 112, 116 (bottom), 118, 119 (top), 121, 122, 132 (middle), 139 (right), 145, 147 (bottom right), 150–1, 159, 160–1, 165, 169, 170–1, 173 175, 176 (top), 178–9, 180–1, 182 (left), 185, 188 (top), 189, 192 (top), 194 (top), 197 (bottom), 198, 203, 205, 209, 214, 215 (bottom), 218, 245, 246, 254 (bottom), 260, 272, 273 (bottom), 278 (bottom right), 279 (inset)

Offside 29, 114–15, 130–1, 133, 134–5, 136, 137 (top), 141 (bottom), 144, 177 (top), 184 (left), 191 (top), 193, 194 (bottom), 197 (top), 278 (top left and top right)

PA Photos 30, 42–3, 46 (top), 47, 51, 65, 72 (bottom), 78 (top), 79, 88–9, 94 (bottom right), 113, 116 (top), 119 (bottom), 142–3, 156 (top), 158, 164 (inset), 172–3, 182–3, 184 (right), 191 (bottom), 224, 229, 230, 232, 264 (bottom), 266, 273 (top), 275, 278 (bottom left), 279

Courtesy of Ivan Ponting 39 (bottom), 46 (bottom), 69 (left), 81 (left), 94 (inset), 131, 156 (middle), 188 (bottom), 200 (bottom)

Rex 44, 223, 256–7, 261

Topfoto 41, 45 (top), 69 (right), 91, 107, 140, 141 (top), 155 (bottom right), 162, 249

Courtesy of Frank Wilson 274 (bottom)